Keepers

Culinary Treasures
from the Heart

JO DUNBAR SNOW

Keepers

ISBN 978-0-615-14089-6

WIMMER
COOKBOOKS

A CONSOLIDATED GRAPHICS COMPANY

800.548.2537   wimmerco.com

These are most favorite, most treasured recipes. They have been created by me, my children, my friends and relatives, by strangers, all of which have been a delight to make and enjoy with exclamations – a Keeper!

Libbie, Amy and Bill grew up as my "assistants" and now I am their "assistant"! Our times in the kitchen preparing our own dinner or for a party are some of the happiest times in my life and bring such joy in remembering. They have their own homes now and are doing the very same thing with their little ones. Their wonderful spouses have certainly added flavors and spice to our festivities!

We love to entertain and although we no longer live in the same town, any future party requires many telephone consultations (we have not resorted to conference calls as yet but I see that coming.) If one of us has created something special, we are immediately on the "hot line"!

What a wonderful way to enjoy one's family and to express our love to each other and our friends.

In the late 1950's and 60's, I wrote a food column for six weekly northern California newspapers. I have included some of these recipes which are "old fashioned" and unsophisticated but are some of my absolute favorites. For instance, the Swedish Meatballs – I must never lose this recipe!

My daughters, Libbie and Amy, live in the Central Valley and often their creative juices produce the most wonderful dishes using the bounty of that area. My son, Bill, is in Seattle and I doubt if I have ever had better barbecued salmon than his.

Warren and I spent so much time in our home in Lake Tahoe. While he was out skiing, chopping wood, fixing, mending, planning, I produced some of our favorite dishes. Such happy, happy days.

As the saying goes - in case of fire, save the photos. I agree, with one addition – save the recipes!

And so, here they are. It is a start and I hope you find each and every recipe herein – a Keeper!

A note: These are either family or friends' recipes which we pass back and forth with each other. They are not "professional, test-kitchen" creations and are merely set down in black and white so that we can reach them more easily than groping through drawers, binders, telephone calls, etc. There are probably some mistakes, but they should be small (hopefully). There are so many more recipes that should be included, but we felt these 250 or so were a good start. Thank you to whomever may have contributed one of these memories.

My family and I dedicate this Collection to all of our friends and each other!

My Favorite Keepers

Name of Recipe	Page

Keepers
TABLE OF CONTENTS

Keepers
NOTES

BEVERAGES

THE MARTINI:

The ultimate combination is a six-to-one blend of London dry gin and French dry vermouth, with a twist of lemon.

The garnish of olive, onion, or lemon is meant to impart a little extra tang.

It should be stirred with a little ice, then strained. Dilution by vigorous shaking with ice defeats the purpose.

THE MANHATTAN:

Combines two parts bourbon, one part sweet vermouth and a dash of bitters. Shake with ice and strain into a glass. A twist of orange or lemon peel and a maraschino cherry adds the classic embellishment.

THE PERFECT MANHATTAN:

Combine two parts bourbon, one-half part sweet vermouth, one-half part dry vermouth. Proceed as above.

THE GIMLET:

Combine four parts gin or vodka with one part Roses lime juice. Shake with ice and strain into a glass. Add a squeeze of fresh lime juice and a lime slice to the glass.

Eggnog

Thank goodness, eggnog appears only once a year! This is just plain delicious.

6 eggs, separated
1 cup sugar
1 pint brandy
½ pint rum
1 quart vanilla ice cream, softened, divided
1 quart half-and-half, divided

Place 3 egg whites in one bowl and the other 3 whites in a second bowl. Place the 6 egg yolks in a third bowl. Beat each bowl of egg whites until they are stiff. Add sugar to egg yolks and mix thoroughly. Add brandy and rum to yolk mixture.

Add half of the ice cream and half of the half-and-half to the egg yolk mixture. Fold in egg whites from first bowl.

Add remaining ice cream and half-and-half to other bowl of egg whites.

Combine the two mixtures.

Golden Glory

Hallelujah! This is smo-o-o-th! This is our Easter morning drink, or sitting-on-the-deck-Tahoe drink, or ladies' luncheon drink, or any excuse drink! It is wonderful. It is sinful!

1 can frozen orange juice concentrate, undiluted
1 juice can gin or vodka
1 juice can half-and-half
1 juice can crushed ice

Pour undiluted juice into a blender. Add gin, half-and-half and ice and whirl in blender until smo-o-o-th!

Serve in champagne glasses.

Margaritas

Never fails to please.

1 lime, cut into wedges
Coarse salt
1 (12-ounce) can frozen limeade
    concentrate
½ can triple sec
½ can fresh lime juice
1 can good quality tequila
Ice

Use one of the lime wedges to rub rims of margarita glasses. Dip rims in coarse salt in a saucer; set aside.

In a pitcher, combine limeade, triple sec, lime juice and tequila. Stir well and fill with ice. When chilled, remove ice and serve in salt-rimmed glasses with a lime wedge.

Sangria

Pretty and pretty delicious – serves 25 or more depending on thirst.

4 (750-ml) bottles Zinfandel wine
½ cup brandy
¼ cup Cointreau
1 quart orange juice
½ cup lemon juice
¼ cup superfine sugar
12 ice cubes
1 quart club soda, chilled
3 oranges, thinly sliced
3 lemons, thinly sliced

Thoroughly chill all ingredients.

Pour wine, brandy and Cointreau into a large punch bowl or glass pitchers.

In a separate container, stir orange and lemon juice with the sugar until sugar dissolves. Add juice mixture to punch bowl and stir to blend.

Add ice cubes and soda and garnish with fruit slices. Serve in 4-ounce punch glasses or wine glasses.

Keepers
NOTES

_____

_____

_____

_____

_____

_____

_____

_____

_____

_____

_____

_____

_____

_____

APPETIZERS

Brie with Sun-Dried Tomatoes and Pesto

Amy introduced us to this great crowd-pleaser – easy to prepare, colorful and tasty.

1 round Brie, any size depending on number of guests
Sun-dried oil-packed tomatoes, finely chopped
Pine nuts
Bottled pesto

Split round of Brie in half horizontally.

Spread chopped sun-dried tomatoes over bottom cheese layer to the edge. Sprinkle with pine nuts. Spread pesto over pine nuts. Place remaining layer of cheese on top.

Serve at room temperature, or place in a 300 degree oven for a few minutes, watching carefully, to soften, but not to melt.

Decorate with a piece of holly, or a pansy, or a small bouquet of parsley in the center. Serve with crackers.

I have successfully frozen leftover slices and simply reheated in oven – as good as new!

Asparagus in Puff Pastry

SERVES 6

My dear friend, Marilyn, introduced us to this outstanding first course – a dish that deserves an "Oscar" as does Marilyn!

1 cup heavy cream

¼ cup minced shallots

¼ cup white wine vinegar

¼ cup white wine

4 teaspoons cold water

2 sticks butter, cut into 16 pieces

Salt and pepper to taste

36 thin asparagus spears, ends peeled

1 sheet puff pastry dough, cut into six (5x2½-inch) rectangles

Egg wash

Preheat oven to 425 degrees.

To make sauce, cook cream in a small pan until reduced to ½ cup.

In a separate heavy pan, combine shallots, vinegar and wine. Reduce to a glaze, watching carefully. Remove from heat and add 4 teaspoons cold water. Whisk in reduced cream. Over very low heat, whisk in butter, one piece at a time, adding one piece just before previous one has completely melted. Season with salt and pepper. Remove from heat, cover and keep warm.

Cook asparagus in boiling water for 6 to 8 minutes. Rinse in cold water, drain and dry with paper towels.

Brush puff pastry with egg wash. Bake 15 minutes or until golden. Transfer to a rack and cool. Cut off top third of each rectangle horizontally to form a lid. Remove any uncooked dough from inside.

To assemble, cut asparagus to fit over rectangles. Place 6 asparagus pieces on each lower portion of rectangles. Nap with sauce and place lid on top. Decorate plates with sprigs of parsley and edible flowers.

Caponata Siciliana

MAKES 4 CUPS

Marilyn is a great cook – she maintains this is the best caponata recipe and we agree. Keep a jar in the refrigerator for an emergency dish or to nibble on for lunch!

1 large eggplant
Salt
1 cup chopped celery
4 tablespoons olive oil, divided
1 onion, chopped
2 teaspoons sugar
3 tablespoons red wine vinegar
1 cup chopped tomato
2 tablespoons slivered black olives
Freshly ground black pepper
1 tablespoon pine nuts

Peel and dice eggplant. Sprinkle with salt and allow to drain in a colander for 30 minutes. Squeeze dry.

Sauté celery in 2 tablespoons olive oil for about 8 minutes. Add onion and sauté another 5 minutes. Remove with a slotted spoon.

Add remaining 2 tablespoons olive oil to pan. Add eggplant and sauté 8 minutes, stirring constantly. Return onion mixture to pan. Add sugar, vinegar, tomato, olives and pepper. Bring to a boil. Reduce heat and simmer, uncovered, for about 10 minutes, stirring frequently.

Transfer mixture to a bowl. Mix in pine nuts. Refrigerate several hours before serving. Keeps well.

Serve with fresh baguette slices.

Cheese Shortbread

Great with drinks or alongside a salad. Good idea to keep an uncooked roll in the freezer for spur-of-the-moment treats.

6 tablespoons butter

½ teaspoon salt

2 egg yolks

¼ teaspoon cayenne pepper

1 cup grated Swiss or Cheddar cheese

1 cup flour

Preheat oven to 350 degrees.

Combine all ingredients in a food processor and mix well.

Remove mixture and press dough together. Roll into a long cylinder. Cut dough into ¼-inch slices and place slices on a baking sheet.

Bake 25 minutes, watching carefully towards the end of baking time. Cool on baking sheet. Remove to a cooling rack.

Chicken Liver Pâté

An old standby that Libbie prepares to perfection.

½ pound chicken livers

Chicken broth

2 hard-cooked eggs

½ cup chopped onion

2 tablespoons butter

Salt and pepper to taste

Pinch of curry powder or dash of cognac

Simmer livers in enough broth to cover for 8 to 10 minutes or until done; drain, reserving cooking liquid. Combine drained livers with eggs in a food processor. Process mixture, using a little of reserved cooking liquid.

Brown onion lightly in butter. Blend onion with liver mixture to make a paste. Season with salt and pepper and curry powder or cognac.

Serve pâté on buttered toast fingers or in a lettuce cup.

Crab Bites

MAKES 72

Cindy always entertains beautifully! She introduced us to these delectable morsels.

I have sometimes not cut the filled halves and served them for a quick and delicious lunch.

1 stick butter, softened
1 cup cooked fresh crabmeat
2 teaspoons mayonnaise
1 tablespoon finely chopped onion
1 clove garlic, finely minced
1 (10-ounce) jar Kraft Old English spread
Dash of black pepper
6 English muffins

Preheat oven to 375 degrees.

Combine all ingredients except English muffins. Split English muffins and spread mixture equally on all halves.

Place muffins on a baking sheet and freeze 30 minutes. Remove from freezer and cut each half into 6 triangles. Can be frozen in freezer bags at this point for future use.

Place triangles on a baking sheet. Bake 15 minutes.

Endive with Herb Cheese

This is one of our old standby nibblies but it never goes out of favor! Arrange the spears around a lovely old piece of China, and in the center place a mound of the sprouts – lacy and inviting.

4 heads Belgian endive
1 package Boursin cheese with herbs, softened
1 tub Alfalfa sprouts

Trim bottoms of endive to separate the leaves. Spread ½ teaspoons of cheese on the bottom of each endive leaf.

Garnish the cheese with sprouts.

Crispy Cashew Oysters

SERVES 6

This recipe deserves 4 stars! The rest of the meal pales when these luscious oysters are served as a first course. This is a true statement!

3 jars fresh Washington oysters, or 24 large plump oysters, shucked with bottom shell reserved

Peanut or vegetable oil for frying

TEMPURA BATTER
½ **cup cornmeal**

½ **cup flour**

1 **teaspoon baking powder**

¼ **teaspoon salt**

⅛ **teaspoon white pepper**

¼-½ **cup ice water**

CASHEW SESAME SAUCE
½ **cup cashews, lightly toasted**

2 **teaspoons black sesame seeds**

2 **teaspoons sesame oil**

2 **teaspoons soy sauce**

2 **tablespoons oyster sauce**

½ **cup rice vinegar**

¼ **cup olive oil**

¼ **teaspoon chopped garlic**

1 **tablespoon honey**

Drain oysters and pat dry; set aside. Heat oil in a deep skillet.

Combine all batter ingredients. Coat oysters with batter, shaking off excess. Fry oysters in hot oil for 1 to 2 minutes or until crisp and brown. If using reserved shells, place oysters on shell and drizzle with sauce.

To make sauce, combine all ingredients and mix well.

I prefer serving oysters over a chiffonade of fresh baby spinach. The warm oysters will slightly wilt the spinach. Top with sauce.

Goat Cheese Spread

Colorful, hearty, addictive – a knockout for a crowd.

**1 pound goat cheese
(buy the creamiest and the best)**

**1 cup sun-dried tomatoes in oil,
well drained**

½ cup capers, rinsed and dried

1 cup Greek olives, pitted

**30 cloves roasted garlic, including
oil in which garlic is cooked
(see below)**

**1 cup roasted red peppers (in jar),
coarsely chopped**

Large leafy greens for garnish

Place cheese on large plate and start piling on drained tomatoes, capers, olives, garlic and peppers. Surround with leaves.

Serve with sliced baguette or crackers.

ROASTED GARLIC:

Place peeled garlic on baking sheet and mix with a generous amount of olive oil. Bake at 350 degrees for about 10 to 12 minutes; do not allow to burn. Test for doneness.

Grilled Prawns with Mint and Feta

Libbie and Amy's specialty, and now yours! A sumptuous appetizer.

½ cup lime juice

½ cup olive oil

Freshly ground pepper

½ cup chopped fresh mint

3 ounces crumbled feta

**2 pounds large prawns, peeled and
butterflied**

Gently combine lime juice, olive oil, pepper, mint and feta in a large bowl.

Grill prawns and add to lime juice mixture.

Decorate with greens and serve with baguette slices.

Goat Cheese with Sun-Dried Tomatoes and Capers

We all agree that this appetizer is hard to beat – everyone literally dives into it! Delicious the next day, if there is any leftover.

12 or more cloves garlic
3 tablespoons extra virgin olive oil
1 (8-ounce) log goat cheese
1 cup sun-dried tomatoes in oil, coarsely chopped
2 teaspoons capers
Freshly ground black pepper
1 teaspoon oregano

Place garlic and oil in a baking pan. Broil until the garlic begins to show brown spots. Remove from oven and cool. Garlic and oil may also be secured tightly in foil and baked at 350 degrees for 30 minutes or until tender.

Slice cheese, keeping the log-shape intact and lay out on serving dish. Sprinkle with chopped tomatoes, capers and pepper. Pour the cooled garlic and oil over all and sprinkle with oregano.

Serve with sliced baguette.

Green Goddess Dip for Crudités

MAKES 2 CUPS

A great dip for veggies – a colorful basket of carrot and celery sticks, radishes, red and yellow pepper strips, asparagus gently blanched, green onions, mushrooms, endive and romaine leaves!

2 ripe avocados, mashed
½ cup sour cream
½ cup mayonnaise
½ cup chopped ripe olives
¼ cup minced green onions
1 can anchovies, drained and minced
1 clove garlic, minced

Combine all ingredients and stir until well blended.

Cover tightly with plastic wrap. Chill several hours to allow flavors to develop. This recipe is easily doubled.

Josefinas

Every member of the family and friends make this easy, delicious appetizer. We all pass it along to the next person who has had it for the first time – they beg for the recipe! Spread the mixture on large slices of French bread and you have a tasty lunch offering.

1 stick butter, softened

1 cup mayonnaise
(light works fine)

2 cups grated Jack cheese

1 (4-ounce) can chopped green
chiles

2 baguettes, cut into thin angled
slices

Whip butter, mayonnaise and cheese in a food processor until smooth. Remove to a bowl and add chiles; do not over mix.

Spread bread slices with cheese mixture. Place on a baking sheet and broil until bubbly – watch carefully!

Decorate with parsley sprigs.

Amy's Olive Tapenade

3 cloves garlic, coarsely chopped

3 tablespoons coarsely chopped
fresh parsley

1 (5-ounce) can black olives,
drained

1 (6-ounce) can kalamata olives,
drained

1 roasted red pepper, chopped

Cracked black pepper

1 tablespoon olive oil

Combine garlic, parsley and both olives in a food processor. Pulse to desired consistency.

Mix in roasted pepper. Add pepper and olive oil.

Famous Amy's Famous Layer Dip

Everyone makes a version of this great party pleaser. This is our favorite combination. Add or delete to it as desired. Each grouping is a layer. Combine the ingredients in each grouping. Use your most colorful large platter and start in!

LAYER ONE
Refried beans
½ cup chunky salsa

LAYER TWO
16 ounces sour cream
1 (1.25-ounce) package taco seasoning

LAYER THREE
6 avocados
Juice of 2 lemon
2 cloves garlic, finely minced
1 tablespoon mayonnaise
2 tablespoons finely chopped red onion
½ teaspoon salt (try to find Jane's Crazy salt)
A few splashes of green taco sauce

LAYER FOUR
Grated Jack cheese
Grated Cheddar cheese

TOPPINGS
Red and green onions, finely chopped
Sliced olives
Chopped tomatoes

Combine ingredients in each layer grouping. Spread first layer over a serving platter. Top with remaining layers in order listed. Sprinkle toppings over all.

Surround with corn or taco chips. Olé!

Miniature Gougères

MAKES ABOUT 3 DOZEN

Heaven is facing a dish of these with a glass of chilled white wine!

1 cup water

1 stick unsalted butter, cut into small pieces

½ teaspoon salt

1 cup flour

4-5 eggs

1½ cups coarsely grated Gruyère cheese

Preheat oven to 375 degrees. Lightly grease 2 baking sheets or line sheets with parchment.

Combine water, butter and salt in a heavy saucepan and bring to a boil. Reduce heat. Add flour all at once and beat with a wooden spoon until mixture pulls away from sides of pan.

Transfer mixture to a bowl. Using an electric mixer on high speed, beat in 4 eggs, one at a time, beating well after each addition. Batter should be stiff enough to just fall off a spoon. If batter seems too stiff, in a small bowl, beat remaining egg lightly and add to batter, a little at a time, until batter is desired consistency. Mix in cheese.

Drop level tablespoons of dough about 1 inch apart on prepared baking sheets. Bake 30 minutes or until puffed, golden and crisp. Check halfway through baking and switch position of sheets.

Phyllo-Wrapped Fried Prawns

SERVES 6

A first course that will "knock their socks off"! Yes, it is a little labor intensive but it is worth every minute it takes to prepare. This dish will make you famous!

3 tablespoons plus 1 stick unsalted butter, divided

2 tablespoons olive oil

24 large prawns, peeled and deveined

¼ cup Sambuca (anise-flavored liqueur)

1 clove garlic, minced

3 tablespoons minced fresh parsley

½ teaspoon dried basil, crumbled

5 sheets phyllo dough, stacked between 2 sheets of wax paper and covered with a damped towel

1½ cups freshly grated Parmesan

½ cup all-purpose flour

3 eggs, lightly beaten

Peanut oil for deep frying

Tomato Anise Sauce (recipe on page 23)

Heat 3 tablespoons butter and oil in a large skillet. Add prawns and sauté, stirring for 2 minutes. Add Sambuca, garlic, parsley and basil and cook 1 minute. Remove from skillet and cool prawns completely in cooking liquid.

In a small saucepan, melt remaining 1 stick butter. Cut the stacked phyllo sheets crosswise into 5 equal strips. Brush a phyllo strip lightly with butter, put 1 prawn on the strip and roll up the shrimp, tucking in the edges to form a package. Working with one phyllo strip at a time, proceed with remaining prawns and butter.

In a small bowl, combine Parmesan and flour. Place beaten egg in a separate small bowl. Dip prawn packages, one at a time, in the egg, letting the excess drip off, then dredge in cheese mixture, patting cheese on gently. Chill on a baking sheet lined with wax paper for 1 hour.

When ready to fry, preheat oven to 250 degrees. Heat 3 inches of peanut oil in a deep skillet to 375 degrees.

PHYLLO-WRAPPED FRIED PRAWNS — CONTINUED

Fry prawn packages, in batches, for 1 to 2 minutes or until golden, turning prawns while frying. Transfer packages to a jelly-roll pan lined with paper towels. Keep warm in oven.

To serve, spoon warm Tomato Anise Sauce onto 6 plates. Arrange 4 prawn packages on each plate. Decorate with sprigs of parsley.

TOMATO ANISE SAUCE

1 onion, chopped

1 tablespoon olive oil

1½ cups dry white wine

½ cup brandy

1 (35-ounce) can diced Italian plum tomatoes, undrained

1½ tablespoons dried basil, crumbled

2 cloves garlic, minced

¼ teaspoon dried thyme, crumbled

1 bay leaf

Pinch of cayenne pepper

½ cup Sambuca

Salt and pepper to taste

In a large saucepan, cook onion in olive oil until softened. Add wine and brandy and cook over high heat until the liquid is reduced by half. Add tomatoes, basil, garlic, thyme, bay leaf and cayenne and bring to a boil. Simmer, stirring occasionally, for 40 minutes.

Add Sambuca and simmer 2 minutes. Discard bay leaf. Cool 10 minutes.

Purée mixture in a food processor and return sauce to pan. Season with salt and pepper and bring to a simmer.

Phyllo Pizza

Elevating pizza to the sublime!

1 stick butter

2 cloves garlic, minced

8 standard size sheets phyllo dough

1½ cups Parmigiano-Reggiano cheese, divided

1 small yellow onion, halved and thinly sliced

10 ripe, but firm Roma tomatocs, thinly sliced crosswise

Handful of chopped fresh herbs or a spoonful of dry mixed herbs

Olive oil

Black pepper to taste

Preheat oven to 400 degrees.

Melt butter with the garlic in a small saucepan.

On a large baking sheet, layer 4 sheets of phyllo, brushing each sheet with garlic butter. Sprinkle with ½ cup cheese.

Layer remaining sheets of phyllo on top, brushing each with garlic butter.

Top with sliced onion and tomatoes, remaining 1 cup cheese and herbs. Drizzle with olive oil and sprinkle with freshly ground black pepper.

Bake until golden in color. Cool slightly before cutting into squares.

Pizza may be assembled a day in advance and baked when needed.

Potato Chip Cheese Cookies

MAKES 24

These were so popular years ago — these are so popular now!

1 stick butter, softened

1 cup grated sharp Cheddar cheese

Dash of Tabasco sauce

2 cups flour

½ cup crushed potato chips

½ cup chopped nuts, optional

Paprika or Parmesan cheese

Preheat oven to 350 degrees.

Combine all ingredients, except paprika or Parmesan.

Form dough into balls. Place balls on a baking sheet and mash down with a fork, scoring twice in opposite directions. Sprinkle with paprika or Parmesan.

Bake about 18 minutes.

Quattro Formagi

Impressive, make-ahead cheese appetizer. Leftovers, if any, make a superb grilled cheese sandwich.

1 (8-ounce) medium-ripe whole Camembert cheese, chilled

1 (3-ounce) package cream cheese, softened

1 (2-ounce) wedge Roquefort, crumbled

1 cup grated Cheddar cheese

1 clove garlic, minced

¼ teaspoon dried basil

¼ teaspoon dried oregano

¼ teaspoon dried rosemary

¼ teaspoon dried thyme

1 tablespoon chopped fresh parsley

2 tablespoons butter, softened

¼ cup thinly sliced green onions

Chill the Camembert. With a sharp knife, cut around top and ¼-inch in from the edge, cutting down about ½ inch into the cheese. With a spoon, carefully scoop out cheese including top rind, leaving a ¼-inch shell intact. Wrap shell and chill. Let remaining cheese warm to room temperature.

Place all remaining ingredients included leftover Camembert in a food processor and mix thoroughly. Mound mixture into shell. Cover and chill at least 1 day or longer.

Let stand at room temperature for 1 hour before serving. Serve with a variety of crackers.

Prawns with Papaya and Prosciutto

SERVES 4

This is a glamorous first course! Most impressive. Be sure to purchase the papaya several days ahead so that it is just right ripe.

1 papaya, peeled, halved lengthwise and seeded

½ pound thinly sliced prosciutto, cut into ½-inch strips

3 tablespoons snipped fresh chives, cut into ½-inch pieces

1 tablespoon fresh lemon juice

4 teaspoons Dijon mustard

Salt and pepper to taste

½ cup extra virgin olive oil

1 pound prawns, shelled, leaving tails intact, rinsed and patted dry

Fresh whole chives for garnish

Cut a papaya half crosswise into 20 thin slices. Arrange 5 slices around the edges of 4 salad plates.

Cut remaining papaya half lengthwise into 2 pieces, then cut it crosswise into thin slices. Gently toss papaya in a bowl with prosciutto and chives.

In a small bowl, whisk together lemon juice, mustard and salt and pepper to taste; set aside.

In a large skillet, heat oil. Add prawns and season with salt and pepper. Cover and cook 2 to 3 minutes, turning occasionally. Using a slotted spoon, transfer prawns to the prosciutto mixture and toss gently. Allow the oil in skillet to cool to lukewarm.

Whisk oil from skillet into lemon juice mixture in a steady stream. Pour lemon sauce over prawn and prosciutto mixture, tossing gently. Adjust seasoning as needed.

To serve, divide mixture equally among the plates. Garnish with a few whole chives.

Quick and Easy Cheese Spreads

A block or two of cream cheese in the refrigerator is the basis for one of these tasty spreads.

SHERRY CHUTNEY CHEESE

1 (8-ounce) package cream cheese, softened

4 ounces sharp Cheddar cheese, grated

2 tablespoons dry sherry

¾ teaspoon curry powder

¼ teaspoon salt

2 drops Tabasco

1 small jar Major Grey's chutney

½ green onion, finely chopped with some of green part

Place cheeses, sherry, curry, salt and Tabasco in a food processor and mix well. Form mixture into a patty about ½-inch thick. Cover and refrigerate overnight.

An hour before serving, remove from refrigerator and top with chutney and green onions. Allow to come to room temperature before serving. Serve surrounded with wheat or sesame crackers.

MOCK BOURSIN

1 (8-ounce) package cream cheese

1 clove garlic, crushed

1 teaspoon caraway seed

1 teaspoon dried basil

1 teaspoon dried dill

1 teaspoon chopped chives

Lemon pepper

Blend all ingredients except lemon pepper. Pat mixture into a patty and roll in lemon pepper.

Shrimp and Goat Cheese Pizza

This is Amy's creation – perfect for lunch or a first course. In lieu of homemade pizza dough, thin type Boboli works just fine. Very pretty, very delicious.

1 large red onion, thinly sliced

1 red bell pepper, thinly sliced

1 yellow bell pepper, thinly sliced

2 tablespoons olive oil, plus extra for brushing on dough

8 cloves garlic, finely minced

1 large thin Boboli

1 cup grated Parmesan or Fontinella cheese

Fresh herbs

1 pound large fresh shrimp, halved lengthwise

Salt and pepper to taste

8 ounces goat cheese, cut into pieces

Preheat oven to 400 degrees.

Sauté onion and peppers slowly in 2 tablespoons oil until soft. Mix in garlic and continue to cook and stir several minutes; cool.

Brush pizza dough with olive oil. Spread vegetable mixture on dough. Sprinkle with grated cheese and herbs. Add shrimp, salt and pepper and goat cheese.

Bake about 10 minutes or until done.

Tomato and Goat Cheese Bruschetta

This is delicious.

1 loaf baguette bread, cut on diagonal into ½-inch slices

7 ounces soft goat cheese

3 tomatoes, finely chopped and drained of juice

1 small red onion, finely chopped

Lightly toast baguette slices. Spread with cheese. Top each slice with 1 tablespoon tomato and 1 teaspoon onion.

Tomato Tapenade

MAKES ABOUT 1½ CUPS

Libbie just "threw" this together one evening. Proof that a well-supplied pantry helps!

1 jar sun-dried tomatoes, packed in oil, drained

½ cup capers, drained

1 can anchovy fillets, drained and chopped

1 clove garlic, finely minced, or more to taste

1 tablespoon finely chopped parsley

2 tablespoons olive oil

1 tablespoon brandy

1 tablespoon Dijon mustard

Blend all ingredients in a food processor.

Delicious on toasted baguette slices.

Triple Cheese Spread

Zesty, but smooth!

1 cup finely shredded Monterey Jack cheese

1 (8-ounce) package cream cheese, softened

⅓ cup Parmesan cheese

1 teaspoon dried thyme

1 teaspoon dried dill

1 clove garlic, minced

2 tablespoons butter, softened

¼ cup dry white wine

Combine all ingredients in a food processor and blend until smooth.

Refrigerate several hours Serve with crackers or as filling in celery.

Domestic Boursin

Just as good as store-bought!

1 (8-ounce) package cream cheese, softened

1 stick butter, softened

½ teaspoon garlic powder

¼ cup Parmesan cheese

2 tablespoons dry white wine

2 tablespoons minced fresh parsley

¼ teaspoon dried marjoram

¼ teaspoon dried thyme

Process all ingredients in a food processor. Chill several hours to allow flavors to blend.

White Bean and Garlic Dip

No need to buy store-bought hummus.

1 (16-ounce) can cannelloni beans, rinsed and drained well

2 cloves garlic, boiled 5 minutes, drained and peeled

1½ tablespoons olive oil

½ teaspoon lemon juice

⅛ teaspoon Tabasco

Salt to taste

Purée all ingredients in a food processor. Serve with pita chips.

Almond Banana Bread

Such a delicious bread! Libbie started making this in the early '80's and we haven't found a better banana bread since.

1 stick butter, softened
1 cup sugar
1 egg
1 teaspoon almond extract
4 ripe bananas, mashed
2 cups flour
½ cup dry cream of wheat
1 teaspoon baking powder
1 teaspoon baking soda
¾ teaspoon cinnamon
¾ teaspoon nutmeg
¼ teaspoon salt
¾ cup almonds, chopped

Preheat oven to 350 degrees.

Beat together butter and sugar until creamy. Add egg and almond extract and beat until fluffy. Mix in bananas.

In another bowl, combine flour, cream of wheat, baking powder, baking soda, cinnamon, nutmeg and salt. Gradually add dry ingredients to creamed mixture, stirring until well blended. Mix in almonds.

Divide batter into 2 loaf pans. Bake 45 to 50 minutes.

Cool in pan 20 minutes, then remove. Serve immediately or wrap and refrigerate.

Makes delicious toast.

If using one large loaf pan, increase baking time to 1 hour.

Breakfast Bake

No one sleeps in when this dish is being served!

12 ounces bulk pork sausage

4 green onions, chopped

2½ cups frozen, loose pack hash brown potatoes

8 ounces Swiss cheese, shredded

1 cup Bisquick baking mix

2 cups milk

⅛ teaspoon pepper

5 eggs

Preheat oven to 400 degrees.

Cook sausage until no longer pink. Drain and pat to remove any fat. Layer sausage, green onions, potatoes and cheese in a greased 9x13-inch baking dish.

Stir together baking mix, milk, pepper and eggs in a large bowl until blended. Pour mixture over layers in baking dish.

Bake, uncovered, for 35 minutes. Cool 5 minutes. Serve with fresh fruit and hot muffins.

Bacon Quiche

This is Amy's standby and should be in everyone's recipe collection. Easily tripled for a crowd.

4 eggs

1½ cups milk

Dash of salt

½ cup Bisquick

4 tablespoons butter, melted

1½ cups shredded Swiss, Cheddar or Jack cheese (or a combination)

9 pieces bacon, cooked and coarsely chopped

Preheat oven to 350 degrees.

Place eggs, milk, salt, Bisquick and melted butter in a blender and mix for 30 seconds. Pour into a greased pie pan. Top with cheese and bacon.

Bake 35 minutes. If doubling or tripling recipe, increase cooking time and size of baking dish accordingly.

M-Bar-J Breakfast Puffs

MAKES 12

Dude ranch vacations are the best! We visited them all and usually came away with at least one recipe from each. This is one of our favorites.

⅓ cup shortening
½ cup sugar
1 egg
1½ cups flour
1½ teaspoons baking powder
½ teaspoon salt
¼ teaspoon nutmeg
½ cup milk

TOPPING
6 tablespoons butter, melted
½ cup sugar
1 teaspoon cinnamon

Preheat oven to 350 degrees.

Cream together shortening, sugar and egg.

In a separate bowl, combine flour, baking powder, salt and nutmeg. Stir dry ingredients into creamed mixture alternately with the milk.

Spoon batter into greased muffin tins, filling each ⅔ full. Bake 20 to 25 minutes.

Remove immediately and add topping by rolling in melted butter, then in a mixture of sugar and cinnamon.

Who needs doughnuts!

Corn Casserole in a Jiffy

Nancy's family recipe – easy and delicious.

1 (11-ounce) can Niblets corn
1 (16-ounce) can creamed corn
1 cup sour cream
¼ cup mayonnaise
1 stick butter, melted
1 (8½-ounce) package Jiffy
cornbread mix
1 cup shredded Cheddar cheese

Preheat oven to 350 degrees.

Combine both cans of corn, sour cream, mayonnaise, melted butter and cornbread mix. Spoon batter into a greased small square glass baking dish.

Bake 20 minutes. Top with Cheddar cheese and bake 10 minutes longer.

This is the original recipe. For a variation, add a small can of diced green chiles and top with grated Mexican cheese mix – olé!

Garlic Bread Bill's Way

Oh my! This is an honest-to-goodness garlic bread!

1 whole head roasted garlic
1 stick unsalted butter, softened
½ cup Parmigiano-Reggiano
cheese
Black pepper
1 loaf Ciabatta bread, halved
lengthwise

Mash roasted garlic in a bowl. Whip in butter, cheese and pepper.

Toast bread halves under a broiler, watching carefully to prevent burning. Spread garlic mixture over toasted bread halves, fold back into a loaf and return to a 200 degree oven to keep warm.

Gee's Pulled Garlic Bread

Gee brought this along to our investment club's Christmas party – this bread was the hit on the buffet table!

1 (1-pound) loaf frozen bread
  dough, thawed

6 tablespoons butter, melted

2 tablespoons chopped fresh sage,
  or 1 tablespoon dried

3 cloves garlic, minced

¼ teaspoon salt

¼ teaspoon freshly ground pepper

¼ teaspoon dried red pepper
  flakes

⅔ cup Parmesan cheese

Cut thawed dough into twelve golf ball-size pieces. Using floured hands, roll each piece into a smooth ball; set aside.

In a small bowl, combine melted butter, sage, garlic, salt, pepper and pepper flakes. Place cheese on a plate.

One at a time, dip each dough ball in butter mixture, then roll in cheese. Place coated balls in generously buttered 9x5-inch loaf pan, fitting 8 balls on the bottom and 4 in the center on top. Pour any remaining butter mixture over the dough.

Let rise until nearly doubled in bulk, which will not take long if dough was at room temperature to start.

When ready to bake, preheat oven to 375 degrees.

Bake 35 to 40 minutes. Cool in pan a few minutes. Remove from pan and serve warm.

Irish Soda Bread

MAKES 2 LOAVES

Libbie's outstanding recipe – we have it annually for St. Pat's Day but it is wonderful any day of the week. Serve with plenty of unsalted butter.

4 cups bread flour

1 tablespoon baking powder

1 teaspoon salt

¾ teaspoon baking soda

1 cup currants, rinsed in hot water and patted dry

2 cups buttermilk

Preheat oven to 350 degrees.

In a large bowl, mix flour, baking powder, salt and baking soda. Stir in currants. Add buttermilk and stir until mixture forms a soft dough.

Turn dough out onto a floured board and knead 1 minute. Using flour hands, halve the dough and shape each half into a round loaf, patting down slightly. Transfer loaves to a lightly greased baking sheet. With a sharp knife, cut an "X" ¼-inch deep across the top of each loaf.

Bake 45 to 55 minutes or until a tester comes out clean. Transfer to a rack and cool.

Leek and Goat Cheese Pie

SERVES 8

An Amy specialty – serve this with a glass of chilled champagne, a crisp salad on the side, and a fruit dessert — a party!

4 tablespoons unsalted butter

6 medium leeks, trimmed, leaving tiny bit of the green, washed, dried and julienned

Salt and pepper to taste

¼ pound pancetta, medium dice

1 egg

½ cup heavy cream

1 teaspoon Dijon mustard

¼ teaspoon curry powder

⅓ pound goat cheese, crumbled, divided

1 sheet puff pastry

½ cup fresh bread crumbs

4 tablespoons butter, melted

Preheat oven to 400 degrees.

Melt butter in a pan. Add leeks and cook 15 minutes or until wilted. Sprinkle with salt and pepper and cover. Continue to cook 10 minutes longer. Set aside to cool.

Meanwhile, fry pancetta 3 minutes or until crispy; do no overcook. Set aside.

Beat egg and cream together. Mix in mustard and curry. Crumble half of the goat cheese into egg mixture. Add cooked leeks and pancetta. Mix well and set aside.

Roll puff pastry into a 10-inch round, about ⅛-inch thick. Transfer pastry to a baking sheet. Roll up pastry around the edge to make a ½-inch deep shell. Place a double thickness of foil around the edge to keep shell in place. Fill shell with leek mixture.

Top with remaining goat cheese and bread crumbs. Drizzle melted butter over all.

Drape a piece of foil over top of pie. Bake 15 minutes. Remove foil, reduce oven temperature to 350 degrees and continue baking 25 to 30 minutes.

Oatmeal Bread

MAKES 2 LOAVES

Another of Amy's hits! Try it – you will love it and your family will adore you, even more!

2 cups boiling water
1 cup rolled oats
½ cup molasses
1 teaspoon butter
1 teaspoon salt
1 heaping tablespoon yeast
  (proofed in ⅓ cup warm water)
5 cups bread flour

Pour boiling water over oats. Add molasses, butter and salt. Stir and cool to lukewarm. When lukewarm, add proofed yeast.

Transfer yeast mixture to the large bowl of an electric mixer. Using a bread paddle and the second to lowest speed, beat in flour until the dough cleans the sides of the bowl.

Turn dough out onto a floured board. If dough is sticky, add a little flour. Knead 1 minute or until smooth.

Place dough in lightly oiled bowl and brush top with oil. Cover with a damp cloth and allow to rise until double. (To hurry process along, heat oven to 200 degrees, immediately turn off oven, and place dough in oven.)

When doubled, punch dough down and allow to rise again. Form into two loaves and place in two greased loaf pans. Rise again.

When ready to bake, preheat oven to 350 degrees.

Bake 35 minutes.

Superb and worth the effort!

Be sure the yeast is fresh! I have learned the hard way that old yeast does not produce a good result. Williams Sonoma carries a very good yeast.

Amy's Corn Chowder

Unbelievable!

½ **pound bacon**
2 red onions, finely chopped
1 bunch green onions, chopped
1 carrot, grated
**6 cups thinly sliced small red
   potatoes**
1 (16-ounce) bag white corn
4 tablespoons butter
¼ **cup flour**
2 (48-ounce) cans chicken broth
2 cups half-and-half
1 tablespoon dried thyme
Salt and pepper to taste

Brown bacon in a stock pot. Drain and chop bacon; set aside. Discard all but 1 tablespoon of the bacon fat in the pot. Add all onions and carrot to pot and sauté until tender; do not brown. Stir in potato and corn.

Meanwhile, melt butter in a saucepan. Stir in flour until smooth to make a roux. Blend roux into sautéed vegetables in pot.

Add broth and half-and-half. Stir in thyme and season with salt and pepper.

Cantaloupe Coconut Soup

A starter of soup always sets the tone for a sit-down dinner. Whether the weather is cold and the soup is hearty or the weather is warm and the soup is cool and refreshing. This soup is truly delicious. It is divine in the middle of summer when cantaloupe is at its peak in sweetness.

2 ripe cantaloupes, peeled and cut into large chunks

¼ cup white wine

½ cup unsweetened coconut milk

½ cup cream

Zest of 1 lime

¼ cup lime juice

½ teaspoon salt

¼ teaspoon black pepper

¼ teaspoon nutmeg

2 tablespoons frozen orange juice concentrate, undiluted

¼ cup shredded coconut, lightly toasted

Purée cantaloupe in a food processor. Add wine, coconut milk, cream, lime zest and juice, salt, pepper, nutmeg and orange juice to processor. Blend well. Adjust seasoning as needed. Chill 2 hours.

To serve, pour into large glasses and sprinkle with toasted coconut.

Chicken and Corn Chowder

Prosciutto and chicken thighs instead of clams and bacon for a different, hearty soup.

3½ ounces prosciutto, chopped

1 onion, chopped

4 cups chicken broth

2 russet potatoes, cut into ½-inch cubes

2 cups corn, fresh or frozen

1 pound boneless, skinless chicken thighs, cut into ½-inch pieces

2 cups half-and-half

1 tablespoons chopped fresh thyme, or 1½ teaspoons dried

Salt and pepper to taste

Sauté prosciutto 3 minutes. Remove prosciutto from pan and set aside. Add onion to pan drippings and sauté until softened, adding butter if mixture is too dry.

Add broth and potato. Cover and simmer 5 minutes.

Add corn and chicken. Partially cover pan and simmer 8 minutes or until chicken is cooked.

Stir in half-and-half and thyme. Season to taste with salt and pepper. Ladle into bowls and sprinkle with reserved prosciutto.

Recipe doubles easily.

Cream of Zucchini Soup

SERVES 4

An old standby and still delicious these many years gone by. I often serve this in the living room as a first course. Very pretty in large goblets. Chinese porcelain spoons are a nice touch.

1 tablespoon butter

1 pound zucchini, unpeeled and thinly sliced

2 tablespoons diced shallots

2 cloves garlic, minced

1 teaspoon curry powder

½ teaspoon salt

½ cup heavy cream

1 (14-ounce) can chicken broth

Chopped chives for garnish

Melt butter in large saucepan. Add zucchini, shallots and garlic. Cover and simmer 10 minutes, shaking the pan now and then to prevent sticking; do not allow vegetables to brown. Remove from stove.

Add curry powder, salt, cream and broth. In several batches, purée in a blender or food processor.

Serve cold with a sprinkling of chopped chives.

Crema Di Pomodoro

SERVES 6-8

This first course soup will outshine the main course!

1 loaf crusty bread, cut into ¼-inch cubes to measure 3 cups

2 carrots, chopped

2 ribs celery, chopped

3 cloves garlic, minced

3 tablespoons olive oil

Crazy Jane salt to taste

1 cup white wine

4½ cups crushed tomatoes

3 cups water, divided

1 cup heavy cream

1 cup sour cream

Pinch of baking soda

1 teaspoon sugar

Salt and pepper to taste

Preheat oven to 350 degrees.

Arrange bread cubes in a single layer on a baking sheet. Bake 25 minutes; set aside.

Sauté carrot, celery and garlic in olive oil for about 20 minutes. Season with Crazy Jane salt. Add wine and boil 3 minutes.

Add crushed tomatoes and 1 cup water. Simmer 20 minutes. Remove from heat. Whisk in heavy cram and sour cream. Cool 15 minutes.

Purée in a blender in batches (use caution with hot liquids). Transfer to a large bowl, then transfer all of purée back to pot. Thin with remaining 2 cups water. Stir in baking soda, sugar and salt and pepper. Correct seasoning as needed.

Heat gently – do not boil. Serve soup ladled over bread croutons in large bowl.

Wonderful!

Five Star Soup

Holiday consumption is telling! Start the New Year (or any other day of the year) with this outstanding vegetable soup. This truly is a "five-star recipe" and will help in absolving our Holiday sins. If you prefer it strictly vegetarian, substitute vegetable broth.

2 cups celery, chopped

1 onion, chopped

1 leek, white-pale green parts, chopped

½ cup white wine

9 cups chicken broth

1 head Chinese cabbage, chopped

2 cups zucchini, diced

½ cup dry pastina

8 ounces spinach, coarsely chopped

½ cup chiffonade fresh basil

Salt and pepper to taste

Parmesan cheese for topping

Combine celery, onion, leek and wine in large pot. Simmer 10 minutes or until just tender.

Add chicken broth and bring to boil. Add cabbage and zucchini and cook 10 minutes. Add pastina and cook 10 minutes. Add spinach and cook 5 minutes.

Season with basil and salt and pepper. Mix well.

Serve in large bowls topped with Parmesan cheese.

French Onion Soup

SERVES 6

This is the best! Better than any we have had in France, better than any we have had in California!

4 tablespoons butter
5 onions, thinly sliced
10 cups canned bouillon soup
3 cloves garlic, finely chopped
Black pepper to taste
24 slices baguette, lightly toasted
1 pound Swiss or Gruyère cheese

Melt butter in a large pot. Add onions and cook on low heat for 15 to 20 minutes or until onions are slightly golden. Add bouillon, garlic and pepper and continue to cook for 30 minutes.

Place 4 slices of bread in each individual ovenproof bowl. Fill bowls halfway with soup. Stop for a bit and then continue adding soup gradually, making sure the bowls are filled to the top.

Sprinkle cheese on top without pushing into the liquid. Press cheese all around the edges of the bowl, so that when it melts it sticks to the sides and forms a crust.

Preheat oven to 400 degrees.

Place bowls in oven and bake about 30 minutes.

Just great!

Oyster Bisque

Trader Vic's was our restaurant of choice for any celebration. Libbie adapted their oyster bisque recipe and we think this is better than the original. An impressive first course!

2 cups milk

1 cup half-and-half

1 jar fresh oysters

1 cup finely chopped fresh spinach

1 clove garlic, minced

1 teaspoon A-1 steak sauce

Salt and pepper to taste

2 tablespoons butter

1 tablespoon cornstarch

1 cup heavy cream, whipped

Heat milk and half-and-half in a saucepan. Add oysters, spinach, garlic, steak sauce, salt and pepper and butter. Bring to simmer but do not boil. Cook for 5 minutes. Remove from heat and allow to cool 5 minutes.

Purée mixture in a blender, in batches, and return to pan.

Combine cornstarch with a little cold water and add to bisque. Heat gently, stirring all the while.

Pour bisque into individual bowls and top with a dollop of the whipped cream. Broil until lightly browned.

Needs no further embellishment!

Shrimp Bisque

SERVES 6

A very delicious, elegant first course! Our Gourmet Group will often decide on an all seafood feast out at Stinson Beach and this is the usual starter. I dare not divulge the remaining items on our menu – decadent! decadent!

4 tablespoons butter

1 onion, finely chopped

3½ cups clam juice

6 tablespoons dry white rice

1 pound peeled and cooked medium prawns, 4 prawns reserved for garnish

3 tablespoons tomato paste

2½ cups half-and-half

Dash of cayenne pepper

Salt and pepper to taste

Finely chopped parsley

Melt butter in a saucepan. Add onion and sauté 5 minutes or until soft.

Add clam juice and rice and bring to boil. Reduce heat and cover. Cook 15 minutes or until rice is tender. Add prawns and heat; do not overcook the prawns.

Cool slightly and purée in batches until smooth. Return bisque to pan.

Add tomato paste, half-and-half and cayenne pepper. Simmer until heated through. Season with salt and pepper.

Serve in individual bowls. Garnish each serving with a reserved prawn and a sprinkling of chopped parsley.

Spanish Beans

Paradors in Spain beg for this recipe!

2 cups extra large white beans

1 ham shank, cut into pieces

1 tablespoon olive oil

1 leek, sliced retaining ½ of green part

2 yellow onions, sliced

8 cloves garlic, minced

1 carrot, coarsely chopped

2 bay leaves

1 tablespoon paprika

2 (14-ounce) cans chicken broth, or more if needed

1 cup half-and-half

Place beans in a saucepan. Cover beans with water and soak overnight.

Drain beans. Add more water to beans to cover by 2 inches. Bring to a boil. Reduce heat and cook 10 minutes. Drain, reserving water.

Sauté ham shank in olive oil until brown. Add leek, onion, garlic and carrot and cook for 30 minutes, stirring occasionally.

Add bay leaves, paprika, drained beans and reserved bean water. Stir in chicken broth and cook, partially covered, for 2½ hours. Add more broth if necessary while cooking. Adjust seasoning as needed.

Add half-and-half and continue to cook until beans are tender.

I sometimes add a bit of chorizo for additional flavor.

Avocado with Tomato and Basil

Ripe avocados, sun-ripened tomatoes, young basil leaves, rosy red onions – our show-stopper standby first course.

1 cup finely chopped red onion

½ cup finely sliced fresh basil leaves

½ cup red wine vinegar

2 cups peeled, seeded and chopped tomatoes

Salt and pepper

1 teaspoon sugar

1 cup olive oil

6 ripe avocados

Blend onion, basil and vinegar in a bowl. Add tomatoes, salt and pepper, sugar and olive oil. Let stand several hours to allow flavors to blend.

Halve the avocados lengthwise and remove the pits. Using a melon baller, scoop out two balls from each hollow; set aside. Make crisscross lines in the remaining flesh.

Heat the dressing gently and spoon into avocado halves. Top with reserved avocado balls. Place on bed of salad greens and serve.

Butter Lettuce and Avocado Salad

Simply delicious!

DRESSING

½ **cup olive oil**

½ **cup vegetable oil**

3 tablespoons minced red onion

1 clove garlic, minced

½ **cup rice vinegar**

1 teaspoon Dijon mustard

½ **teaspoon celery salt**

SALAD

2 packages butter lettuce and
    radicchio mix

3 avocados, peeled and sliced

½ **red onion, finely chopped**

Baby tomatoes, mixed colors

Combine all dressing ingredients in a covered jar. Allow to stand at room temperature for 24 hours. Refrigerate dressing 1 hour before serving.

For salad, place lettuce mix on a flat serving place. Arrange avocados symmetrically on top. Place onion in center and garnish with tomatoes.

When ready to serve, pour dressing over salad and mix.

Caesar Salad I

Unconventional yes, but oh, so delicious!

¾ cup mayonnaise

3 cloves garlic

1 (2-ounce) can rolled anchovies
  with capers

2 tablespoons Parmigiano-
  Reggiano cheese, plus extra for
  topping

1 tablespoon lemon juice

1 teaspoon Worcestershire sauce

1 teaspoon Dijon mustard

Salt and pepper to taste

1 large head romaine lettuce, cut
  into bite-size pieces

Croutons (recipe below)

Place mayonnaise and garlic in a food processor and blend. Add anchovies, cheese, lemon juice, Worcestershire sauce, mustard and salt and pepper. Blend.

Place lettuce in a serving bowl. Add enough dressing to coat. Add extra cheese and croutons. Toss gently.

CROUTONS

4 cloves garlic, halved

¼ cup olive oil

4 cups (¾-inch) bread cubes,
  crusts removed

Sauté garlic in olive oil in a skillet for 1 minute; discard garlic. Add bread cubes to oil in skillet and sauté 15 minutes or until golden brown.

Caesar Salad II

SERVES 8

2 cloves garlic, minced

Pinch of salt

¼ cup fresh lemon juice

2 tablespoons Worcestershire sauce

2 teaspoons Dijon mustard

6 tablespoons sour cream

½ teaspoon freshly ground pepper

1 cup olive oil

⅔ cup freshly grated Parmigiano-Reggiano cheese

Romaine lettuce, torn into bite-size pieces

Croutons (page 51 or page 53)

In a large bowl, make a paste of the garlic and salt. Add lemon juice, Worcestershire, mustard, sour cream and pepper.

Whisk in oil in steady stream until dressing is emulsified. Stir in cheese.

Add lettuce and croutons and toss.

Caesar Salad III

Here is the Classic!

1 cup freshly grated Parmigiano-
  Reggiano cheese, divided

8 anchovy filets, minced

3 tablespoons fresh lemon juice

3 cloves garlic, minced

1 tablespoon Dijon mustard

¾ cup olive oil

Salt and pepper to taste

Romaine lettuce hearts, torn into
  bite-size pieces

1 cup croutons (recipe below)

½ cup Reggiano Parmesan

Combine ½ cup cheese, anchovies, lemon juice, garlic and mustard in a food processor. With processor running, slowly add olive oil. Season with salt and pepper.

Place lettuce in a large bowl. Drizzle with two-thirds of dressing. Top with croutons and some of remaining ½ cup cheese. Toss to mix.

Serve, passing remaining dressing and cheese on the side.

CROUTONS

3 tablespoons olive oil

4 cloves garlic, minced

1 teaspoon dried thyme

Sour dough bread slices, crust cut
  off, cut into ¾-inch cubes

Preheat oven to 350 degrees.

Heat oil and garlic together. Add thyme. Combine with bread cubes. Place on a baking sheet and toast in oven 10 to 15 minutes.

My Best Chicken Salad

Ladies' luncheon fare at its best!

1 (8-ounce) can pineapple chunks, drained, juice reserved
⅔ cup mayonnaise
1 tablespoon Dijon mustard
1 teaspoon curry powder
⅛ teaspoon salt
4 cups chopped cooked chicken
½ cup thinly sliced celery
2 tablespoons finely chopped green onions
⅓ cup slivered almonds, lightly toasted
⅓ cup raisins or currants
Lettuce
Fresh fruit
Major Grey's chutney

Mix drained pineapple, 2 tablespoons reserved pineapple juice, mayonnaise, mustard, curry powder and salt; set aside.

Combine chicken, celery, green onions, almonds and raisins in a separate bowl. Blend in mayonnaise mixture. Refrigerate at least 1 hour, preferably longer.

Serve chicken salad on lettuce, garnished with fresh fruit and topped with a dollop of chutney.

Chutney Salad Dressing

Libbie's best!

¾ cup olive oil
½ cup mango chutney
6 tablespoons white wine vinegar
1 tablespoon Dijon mustard
1 tablespoon soy sauce
1 tablespoon sesame oil
¼ teaspoon crushed red pepper flakes
2 cloves garlic, chopped
½ teaspoon salt

Combine all ingredients in a food processor and purée.

Three-Layered Christmas Salad

SERVES 12

No Christmas buffet should be without this beautiful salad.

2 (1-ounce) packages raspberry gelatin

2 (10-ounce) packages frozen raspberries, thawed and drained, juice reserved

1 (8-ounce) package cream cheese, softened

1 cup chopped walnuts

2 (1-ounce) packages lime gelatin

2 (11-ounce) cans Mandarin oranges, drained, juice reserved

Prepare raspberry gelatin according to package directions, using reserved raspberry juice and adding hot water to equal 4 cups liquid. Chill slightly and fold in thawed raspberries. Pour gelatin into an 8-cup ring mold. Refrigerate until firmly jelled.

Beat cream cheese until fluffy. Fold in walnuts. Carefully spread cream mixture over raspberry gelatin layer.

Make lime gelatin according to directions, using reserved Mandarin orange juice and adding hot water to equal 4 cups liquid. Chill slightly and fold in Mandarin oranges. Refrigerate. When slightly jelled, carefully spread over the cream cheese layer. Refrigerate overnight.

To serve, unmold onto a serving plate and surround with greens.

Very festive!

Curried Pea Salad

My version of this favorite salad. Every time I serve it, the recipe is requested.

Great on a buffet table or a wonderful side dish at a BBQ. Delicious the next day – if there are any leftovers. Easily doubled.

¾-1 cup mayonnaise

1½ teaspoons curry powder

½ teaspoon garlic powder

Salt and pepper to taste

2 (16-ounce) bags petite frozen peas, defrosted

1 cup slivered almonds

Combine mayonnaise, curry, garlic powder and salt and pepper. Mix in peas and almonds.

Refrigerate until needed.

Endive and Walnut Salad

SERVES 6

Fantastic combination of flavors and textures – elegant! Great first course for a "company dinner" and can be prepared early in the day.

6 tablespoons walnut or olive oil

2 tablespoons minced green onions

2 teaspoons Dijon mustard

1½ teaspoons sugar

1 small Red Delicious apple, peeled and finely cubed

Salt and pepper to taste

6 large Belgian endive leaves, unwashed

3 tablespoons coarsely chopped walnuts

3 tablespoons Roquefort or Gorgonzola cheese

Combine oil, green onions, mustard, sugar and apple in a salad bowl. Whisk until thoroughly blended. Season with salt and pepper.

Break endive into salad bowl over dressing; do not mix. Add walnuts and cheese. Chill.

Just before serving, toss salad and arrange on individual serving plates.

Do not wash endive as washing gives a bitter flavor.

Fresh Cranberry Salad

Our traditional Christmas salad – crisp, refreshing, beautiful.

2 (1-ounce) packages raspberry
  gelatin

2 cups crushed pineapple,
  drained, juice reserved

2 tablespoons sugar

2 cups ground fresh cranberries
  (pulse in processor)

2 cups walnut meats, chopped

2 cups chopped celery

Make gelatin according to package directions, using reserved pineapple juice and adding hot water to equal 4 cups liquid. Chill until wobbly.

Fold in crushed pineapple, sugar, cranberries, walnuts and celery. Pour gelatin into an 8-cup ring mold. Refrigerate overnight.

Unmold and decorate with greens – holly is a very nice touch.

Holiday Salad

This salad could not be prettier!

4 oranges, peeled and divided into
  sections

4 avocados, sliced

Green leaf lettuce

DRESSING

1 (16-ounce) can cranberry sauce

2 heaping tablespoons mayonnaise

2 tablespoons lemon juice

Arrange orange and avocado slices alternately in a fan shape on lettuce.

Combine all dressing ingredients. Drizzle dressing decoratively onto fruit.

Fuyu Persimmon and Arugula Salad

A copy of this recipe is requested every time I serve it to guests. It is beautiful to taste and to see! I often times double or triple the recipe and present it as a composed salad.

1 shallot, minced

2 tablespoons sherry wine vinegar or freshly squeezed lemon juice

1 fresh thyme sprig

½ cup olive oil

Salt and pepper to taste

1 cup pecans

2 tablespoons sugar

Cayenne pepper to taste

3 Fuyu persimmons, peeled and sliced

2 small handfuls arugula

2 small handfuls red oak leaf lettuce

2 pomegranates, seeds removed from peel

8 ounces goat cheese, crumbled

Soak shallots in vinegar with thyme for 25 minutes. Whisk in olive oil and season with salt and pepper.

Preheat oven to 375 degrees.

Blanch pecans in boiling water for 5 minutes; drain. Toss pecans with sugar and cayenne. Spread on a baking sheet and toast in oven for 20 minutes or until crunchy. Cool pecans and coarsely chop.

Toss persimmons and pecans in a bowl with some of the vinaigrette.

Add arugula and lettuce and gently toss again, adding more vinaigrette.

Arrange salad on individual plates. Sprinkle with pomegranate seeds and crumbled goat cheese.

During the season, Trader Joe's sells fresh pomegranate seeds in small containers.

Horseradish Beet Salad

This is another of my '50's specials. Beets are "in" again – perhaps dress this up with a sprinkling of goat cheese, a few chopped walnuts and voilá, a 21st century new salad! Colorful, tasty, zesty!

1¾ cups juice from beets, heated (It may be necessary to add water to total 1¾ cups.)

1 (1-ounce) package lemon gelatin

1 tablespoon vinegar

½ teaspoon salt

1 teaspoon grated onion

3 tablespoons bottled horseradish

⅔ cup diced celery

1 (16-ounce) can diced beets, drained

Mix beet juice with gelatin. Add vinegar and salt. Cool until slightly jelled.

Stir in onion, horseradish, celery and beets. Pour mixture into a mold and chill.

Horseradish Mold

There are some things that are apt to date someone – like this 50's gelatin (wrinkles and gray hair does the same thing!) This old goodie has always been a favorite to serve alongside baked ham or roast tenderloin. It was always part of the Fairmont Hotel's sumptuous brunch. Delicate to behold, refreshing to the palate!

1 (3-ounce) package lemon gelatin

1 cup boiling water

¼ teaspoon salt

2 tablespoons fresh lemon juice

1 cup heavy cream

¾ cup drained bottled horseradish

Combine gelatin, boiling water, salt and lemon juice. Chill until slightly jelled.

Whip the cream until stiff. Fold cream and horseradish into gelatin and pour into a mold. Chill until firm. Can be made a day in advance.

Lemon Lime Soufflé Salad

No collection of special recipes would be complete without this favorite – sublime.

1 (1-ounce) package lemon gelatin
1 (1-ounce) package lime gelatin
2 cups hot water
2 cups crushed pineapple, undrained
2 tablespoons lemon juice
1 cup whipped cream
1 cup small curd cottage cheese
1 tablespoon bottled horseradish
1 cup chopped walnuts
1 cup mayonnaise

Mix both gelatins with hot water until dissolved. Chill until slightly firm.

Combine undrained pineapple, lemon juice, whipped cream, cottage cheese, horseradish, walnuts and mayonnaise. Gently fold pineapple mixture into gelatin. Pour into a mold and chill until firm.

For a milder version of this salad, horseradish and walnuts can be omitted – different but equally delicious.

Old-Fashioned Potato Salad

This is a mushy potato salad that everyone loves.

10 potatoes, unpeeled
Salt and pepper to taste
3 green onions
2 hard-boiled eggs
6 sprigs parsley
1 stalk celery
1 cup mayonnaise, or more if needed
½ cup sweet pickle relish
1 (2¼-ounce) can chopped olives
1 (2-ounce) jar pimiento, finely chopped

Cook potatoes until done. Peel and cube the potatoes while still warm, allowing the potatoes to crumble a bit. Place potatoes in a large bowl and season with salt and pepper.

Combine onions, eggs, parsley, celery and mayonnaise in a food processor. Blend until well mixed.

Add mayonnaise mixture to potatoes. Stir in pickle relish, olives and pimiento.

Marinated Mushrooms and Avocados

SERVES 4-6

A hearty salad – a perfect accompaniment to grilled fish or sizzling steak.

¾ cup salad oil

3 tablespoons white wine vinegar

3 tablespoons fresh lemon juice

2 cloves garlic, minced

2 tablespoons chopped fresh
   parsley

1 teaspoon salt

1 teaspoon dried marjoram

1 teaspoon sugar

½ teaspoon dry mustard

½ teaspoon paprika

¼ teaspoon freshly ground pepper

1 pound mushrooms, sliced

2 avocados

Butter lettuce

½ cup cherry tomatoes, halved

Combine oil, vinegar, lemon juice, garlic, parsley, salt, marjoram, sugar, mustard, paprika and pepper. Transfer mixture to a heavy plastic bag. Add mushrooms, gently stirring to coat. Seal bag and refrigerate overnight.

About 1 hour before serving, peel, seed and cut avocados into slices. Add avocado to mushroom mixture, gently stirring to coat.

With a slotted spoon, transfer mixture to a serving dish lined with lettuce. Scatter tomato halves on top.

Panzanella

SERVES 4

Bright red and juicy ripe, one could make a meal on this favorite Italian bread and tomato salad.

½ **pound coarse bread, 3 or 4 days old**

½ **cup water**

1 **cucumber, cut into ½-inch cubes**

4 **ripe tomatoes, diced**

1 **red onion, diced**

½ **cup basil, julienned**

5 **tablespoons red wine vinegar**

2 **cloves garlic, minced**

½ **cup olive oil**

Salt and pepper to taste

Place bread in a bowl. Pour water over bread and allow to sit 2 minutes. Squeeze out water.

Combine drained bread with cucumber, tomato, onion, basil, vinegar, garlic, olive oil and salt and pepper.

Double this recipe – everyone wants seconds!

Rice Shrimp Salad

This is our dear friend, Sue's, famous salad. It is the kind of salad you just cannot stop eating! Double or triple the recipe since everyone will want seconds or thirds!

1 **cup small cooked shrimp**

½ **cup finely chopped red bell pepper**

⅓ **cup finely chopped fresh parsley**

2 **cups cooked rice**

1 **cup mayonnaise**

1 **(10-ounce) package frozen tiny peas, thawed**

Salt and pepper to taste

Combine all ingredients. Cover and refrigerate several hours.

Pear and Cheese Salad

SERVES 4

Pam is a wonderful cook! She tries anything and everything and thinks nothing of preparing sumptuous lunches for 100 – always something new and different with many different dishes. This recipe is one of her discoveries and I believe it to be one of the most innovative and delicious salads I have ever eaten and prepared.

1 loaf baguette bread, very thinly sliced

Olive oil

Parmesan cheese

4 tablespoons butter

1½ tablespoons brown sugar

½ teaspoon cracked black pepper, plus extra for topping

1 tablespoon chopped fresh cilantro

2 pears, not too soft, peeled and sliced

Fresh arugula

1 English cucumber, thinly sliced

1 red onion, thinly sliced, the rings soaked in cold water several hours

8 tablespoons Stilton cheese, crumbled

Brush baguette slices with olive oil and sprinkle with Parmesan. Broil until golden and crisp, watching every second!

Melt butter with brown sugar, pepper and cilantro in a large skillet and mix with a wooden spoon. Add pear slices and cook on each side for about 2 minutes.

Arrange arugula, cucumber slices and onion rings on a plate. Top with sautéed pears and any juices remaining in skillet.

Sprinkle with Stilton cheese and additional cracked pepper.

Unusual, but absolutely delicious!

Double the butter, brown sugar and cilantro for more sauce, if desired.

Potato Caesar Salad

An old favorite.

DRESSING
1 egg
3 anchovies
2 cloves garlic, minced
¼ cup lemon juice
½ cup Parmesan cheese
½ cup vegetable oil
Salt and pepper to taste

SALAD
8 cups large cubed potatoes
⅓ cup sliced green onions
¼ cup minced fresh parsley
Romaine lettuce leaves

For dressing, combine egg, anchovies, garlic, lemon juice, cheese, vegetable oil and salt and pepper in a blender. Process until smooth.

Cook cubed potatoes in boiling water for 10 minutes or until done; drain and cool. Place cooled potatoes in a bowl.

Add dressing to potatoes. Mix in green onions and parsley. Chill 2 hours.

Place salad on a large platter. Slip romaine leaves around edges.

Salad Dressing with Many Vinegars

A light dressing over Shrimp Louis for a change. Try with a mixture of mixed greens, diced tomato, avocado, sliced green onions and sliced English cucumber. Or, any salad!

⅓ cup rice vinegar
⅓ cup sherry vinegar
⅓ cup balsamic vinegar
1 clove garlic, minced
½ teaspoon curry powder
1 teaspoon salt
Freshly ground pepper to taste
1 cup olive oil

Combine all vinegars, garlic, curry powder, salt and pepper in a food processor and blend.

With motor running, slowly add olive oil and process until well blended.

Red Cabbage Salad

Or jaw breaker salad as my friend MJ calls it! Nutritious, delicious.

SALAD

1 head red cabbage, finely shredded

1 apple, unpeeled and diced

½ cup chopped walnuts

½ cup raisins

3 tablespoons Gorgonzola, crumbled

1 bunch green onions, finely sliced

DRESSING

½ cup white vinegar, or mix white with balsamic vinegar

⅔ cup salad oil

2 tablespoons finely chopped mango chutney

1 teaspoon curry powder

1 teaspoon salt

1 teaspoon dry mustard

Several dashes of Tabasco sauce

Combine all salad ingredients in a large bowl and mix well.

Combine all dressing ingredients in a jar and shake vigorously.

Pour dressing over salad and toss to mix well.

For variety, try using green cabbage and substituting pine nuts for the walnuts.

Shrimp and Avocado Salad

SERVES 4

This is such a simple salad and so often forgotten. Good rolls and a pretty dessert – what more for a happy ladies' luncheon!

1 cup mayonnaise
½ cup chopped green onions
½ cup chopped fresh parsley
2 tablespoons lemon juice
1 teaspoon sugar
¼ teaspoon salt
1 pound small cooked shrimp
2 ripe avocados
Tomato wedges and garden fresh greens for garnish

Combine mayonnaise, green onions, parsley, lemon juice, sugar, salt and shrimp. Refrigerate 2 hours.

To serve, halve avocados. Spoon shrimp salad onto avocado halves. Garnish with tomato wedges and greens.

Warren's Favorite Salad Dressing

Poker night once a month with his buddies of a half-century and dinner at the White Horse in San Francisco. The generous chef finally shared this outstanding recipe so that Warren could have it more often at home – with me!

1 medium egg
½ red onion, chopped
⅔ cup raspberry vinegar
⅓ cup sugar
1 teaspoon salt
2 cups canola oil
Mixed salad greens
Crumbled blue cheese

Combine egg, onion, vinegar, sugar and salt in a blender and process. With motor running, drizzle in oil.

Serve vinegar dressing with mixed greens and top with crumbled blue cheese.

Vinaigrette for Green Beans or Asparagus

A festive veggie on a buffet table – we once multiplied the ingredients by 10 and served 150 guests

3 pounds green beans or asparagus

VINAIGRETTE
1 dill pickle, finely minced
2 tablespoons finely minced green onion
1 tablespoon minced capers
1 teaspoon salt
½ teaspoon black pepper
1 teaspoon dry mustard
¼ cup wine vinegar
1 tablespoon lemon juice
1 cup olive oil
1 tablespoon chopped fresh parsley
1 tablespoon minced pimiento
2 hard-cooked egg whites, minced

Steam green beans or asparagus until tender; do not overcook. Transfer to a bowl.

Meanwhile, combine all vinaigrette ingredients. Pour vinaigrette over vegetables.

If dressing is made ahead, add the parsley, pimiento and egg white just before serving.

White Corn Salad

A great buffet dish. Refreshing and simple. Libbie started it and we all continue in her Corn Salad tradition!

DRESSING

¾ cup olive oil

⅓ cup fresh lemon juice

1 teaspoon Worcestershire sauce

6 dashes of Tabasco sauce

2 cloves garlic, crushed

Salt and pepper to taste

SALAD

2 (16-ounce) packages frozen white corn

½ red onion, finely chopped

1 tablespoon chopped fresh rosemary

Cherry tomatoes, quartered

Combine all dressing ingredients in a food processor; set aside.

For salad, cook corn as directed on package; drain and cool.

Mix drained corn and onion in a bowl. Pour dressing over mixture. Add rosemary and tomatoes and toss to mix.

Wild Rice Salad

A perfect buffet dish.

1 cup dry wild rice, rinsed
5½ cups chicken broth
1 cup pecans, coarsely chopped
1 cup golden raisins
Zest of 1 orange
4 green onions, thinly sliced
¼ cup olive oil
⅓ cup orange juice
1½ teaspoons salt
Black pepper to taste

Combine rinsed rice and broth in a saucepan. Bring to a boil. Reduce heat and simmer, uncovered, for 45 minutes or until rice is tender. Drain, if necessary.

Mix cooked rice with pecans, raisins, orange zest, green onions, olive oil, orange juice, salt and pepper. Let stand 2 hours to develop flavors.

Easily doubled. Any leftovers can be used to stuff Cornish hens for roasting.

Zesty Shrimp Salad

SERVES 8

A refreshing summer salad.

DRESSING
- 1¼ cups salad oil
- ¼ cup malt vinegar
- ¼ cup red wine vinegar
- 2½ tablespoons Worcestershire sauce
- 1 tablespoon dry mustard
- 1½ teaspoons salt
- 1 teaspoon freshly ground pepper
- 2½ tablespoons finely chopped red onion
- 2½ tablespoons finely chopped fresh parsley
- 2½ tablespoons capers, rinsed and finely chopped
- ½ cup pickle relish

SALAD
- 2 pounds small cooked shrimp
- Butter lettuce
- Tomatoes, peeled and cut into wedges

Combine all dressing ingredients. Refrigerate 2 hours.

To assemble salad, arrange shrimp on a bed of lettuce. Surround with tomato wedges. Drizzle dressing over salad.

Baked Salmon with Cucumber Sauce

Especially delicious!

⅓ **cup white wine**

⅓ **cup lemon juice**

⅓ **cup soy sauce**

6 (6-ounce) salmon fillets with skin

Mix wine, lemon juice and soy sauce in 9x13-inch glass baking dish.

Place salmon in dish, flesh-side down. Cover with plastic wrap and refrigerate 2 hours, turning occasionally.

Preheat oven to 450 degrees.

Shake excess marinade off salmon and place on a foil-lined baking sheet. Roast about 12 to 14 minutes.

Season salmon and top with dollops of Cucumber Sauce. Serve with steamed baby red potatoes – yum when they are rolled in the sauce.

CUCUMBER SAUCE

1 cup spinach leaves

1 cup arugula leaves

½ **shallot**

¾ **cup sour cream**

1 tablespoon Dijon mustard

½ **cup peeled, seeded and chopped English cucumber**

To make sauce, process spinach, arugula, shallot, sour cream and Dijon mustard in a food processor until well blended. Stir in cucumber. Adjust seasoning as needed.

Baked Halibut

Perfect every time.

1 tablespoon lemon juice
½ cup mayonnaise
3 green onions, thinly sliced
2 tablespoons Parmesan cheese
4 halibut steaks
Bread crumbs

Preheat oven to 400 degrees.

Mix lemon juice, mayonnaise, green onions and cheese.

Spread mixture on halibut and sprinkle with generous amount of bread crumbs.

Bake about 12 minutes.

King Crab Legs

SERVES ABOUT 4, DEPENDING ON APPETITES!

This is one of our newest recipes, planned for the next collection but I could not resist sharing this a.s.a.p.! The fish monger at Costco "explained" this recipe to Libbie and me and we perfected it!

1 stick butter
½ cup olive oil
8 cloves garlic, chopped
Dried red pepper flakes
4 pounds king crab legs
Chopped Italian parsley
Lemon wedges

Preheat oven to 400 degrees.

Melt butter with olive oil in a baking pan. Add garlic and pepper flakes.

Add crab legs and bake 15 minutes.

Sprinkle with parsley and garnish with lemon wedges. Serve with crusty bread to dip into the wonderful garlic butter drippings.

This is an expensive dish but worth every cent!

Crab Cakes

MAKES 6

A delicate crab-y crab cake. A first course or luncheon dish.

½ teaspoon dry mustard

¼ teaspoon ground white pepper

¼ teaspoon cayenne pepper

¼ teaspoon Old Bay seasoning

½ teaspoon Worcestershire sauce

1 tablespoon chopped fresh parsley

½ cup mayonnaise

1½ pounds crabmeat

1 egg, beaten

2 tablespoons cracker meal or bread crumbs, or as needed

Vegetable oil for frying

Combine mustard, white pepper, cayenne, Old Bay seasoning, Worcestershire sauce, parsley and mayonnaise and mix well.

Add crabmeat, egg and cracker meal. Add extra cracker meal, if needed, for the mixture to just hold together. Form into 6 cakes. Refrigerate 30 minutes.

Preheat oven to 400 degrees.

Heat oil in a skillet. Sear cakes in hot oil on both sides. Transfer to a baking sheet and finish in oven for 10 minutes.

Serve on field greens with a dollop Mustard Mayonnaise

MUSTARD MAYONNAISE

1 tablespoon rice vinegar

1 tablespoon dry mustard

1 teaspoon Worcestershire sauce

1 cup mayonnaise

Combine all ingredients and mix well. Refrigerate until needed.

Dunbar's Dandy Sauce

Robert's specialty – always made with pomp and ceremony! Perfect for these fail-proof prawns.

1 cup mayonnaise
½ cup ketchup
¼ cup bottled horseradish
1 teaspoon Dijon mustard
½ teaspoon celery salt
½ teaspoon thyme
½ teaspoon curry powder
Dash of Tabasco sauce
½ teaspoon Worcestershire sauce

Mix together all ingredients – it is a dandy!

BOILED PRAWNS

Taneya was a wonderful Japanese cook who helped us with parties many years ago. This is her method.

2 pounds large prawns

Bring a pot of well-salted water to a boil. Add prawns and simmer while bringing water to a boil again. Immediately remove prawns from water and drain.

When cool, peel, then chill until serving.

Layered Cioppino

Royalty is coming to dinner! Budget breaker, yes, but history-making!

2 (26-ounce) cans whole tomatoes

1 (6-ounce) can tomato paste

1 cup dry white wine

¼ cup olive oil

½ teaspoon black pepper

10 ounces Swiss chard, coarsely chopped

2 red bell peppers, chopped

½ cup chopped fresh parsley

¼ cup chopped fresh basil

2 tablespoons chopped fresh marjoram, or 1 tablespoon dried

2 tablespoons chopped fresh thyme, or 1 tablespoon dried

2 tablespoons chopped fresh sage, or 1 tablespoon dried

3 dozen small clams, scrubbed

3 dozen jumbo shrimp, deveined

2 large dungeness crabs, cracked

2 pounds firm white fish or sea scallops

Mash tomatoes in a bowl. Stir in tomato paste, wine, oil, pepper, chard, bell pepper, parsley, basil, marjoram, thyme and sage.

Arrange clams in the bottom of a 14-quart pot. Spoon ¼ cup of tomato mixture over clams. Layer shrimp, ¼ cup tomato mixture, crabs, ¼ cup tomato mixture, fish and remaining tomato mixture.

Cover pot tightly and boil 10 to 15 minutes. Reduce heat and simmer 15 to 20 minutes.

To serve, dig deep and ladle into large bowls.

Mussel Achievement

The best mussels – after trying them all!

2 shallots, chopped

2 tablespoons olive oil

1 rib celery, chopped

6 green onions, sliced

Dash of curry powder

½ teaspoon fine herbs

1 cup dry vermouth or white wine

2 (6-ounce) cans chopped clams, drained, liquid reserved

½ cup heavy cream

4 pounds mussels

Chopped fresh parsley for garnish

Sauté shallots in olive oil for 2 minutes. Add celery and green onions and cook 2 minutes. Add curry and fine herbs. Stir in vermouth and reserved clam juice. Cook 4 minutes.

Add cream and mussels. Cover and cook until all mussels open.

Add clams. Cook and stir until heated. Serve in deep bowls sprinkled with chopped parsley.

Wonderful over cooked pasta. Crusty bread as an accompaniment is a must!

Paella

SERVES 8

I have been making paella for years. My first successful endeavor called for finishing the dish in the oven, but thanks to a friend who truly knows his paella, the whole enterprise occurred atop the stove. The completed dish must have an almost burnt crust on the bottom. A good paella pan is a must, as is a good Spanish Roja!

1 yellow onion, chopped

Olive oil

2 red bell peppers, finely diced

4 cloves garlic, finely chopped

10 green onions, sliced on the diagonal, green part sliced and reserved for garnish

2 pounds boneless, skinless chicken thighs, cut into small pieces

4 mild Italian sausages, casings removed and cut into bite-size pieces

2 cups dry Arborio or Spanish paella rice

1 cup white wine

1 package saffron threads

Dash of dried red pepper flakes

3 (14½-ounce) cans chicken broth

2 pounds large prawns, peeled

2 pounds mussels, debearded (discard any open mussels)

2 pounds small clams

½ (10-ounce) package frozen small peas

Lemon slices for garnish

Using large paella pan, sauté yellow onion in olive oil until just soft, but not browned. Add bell pepper, garlic and green onions and sauté until soft. Remove all and set aside.

Add chicken to paella pan and sauté until slightly browned. Remove and set aside. Sauté sausage until cooked. Remove and set aside.

Add 2 tablespoons olive oil, if needed, to the pan. Sauté rice until very light in color. Add wine, saffron and pepper flakes and stir well. Add chicken broth and stir.

At this point, stop stirring the rice. Add sautéed vegetables, cooked chicken and sausage, prawns, mussels and clams, pushing the meat and seafood down into the rice mixture.

Cook on high for 25 to 30 minutes or until rice is tender and the bottom crust is almost burnt.

Add peas and sprinkle the reserved sliced green onion tops over all. Decorate the pan with lemon slices.

Pecan-Crusted Salmon with Spinach Sauce

SERVES 4

Prep can be done ahead of time, which makes this a great dish for entertaining. My diary/recipe book states "this is the best salmon I have ever cooked" and it is!

SPINACH SAUCE

½ **cup packed finely chopped spinach**

2 **tablespoons white wine**

1 **tablespoon minced shallots**

1 **cup heavy cream**

1 **tablespoon fresh lime juice**

Salt and white pepper to taste

SALMON

½ **cup pecans**

1½ **teaspoons chopped fresh tarragon**

1½ **teaspoons chopped fresh basil**

1 **tablespoon butter, softened**

4 **(6- to 8-ounce) salmon fillets, skinned (can be cut into portions after baking)**

Salt and pepper to taste

To make sauce, combine spinach, wine and shallots in small, heavy saucepan. Stir over medium heat for 2 minutes or until spinach wilts. Add cream and lime juice and cook until sauce consistency is reduced. Cool to warm temperature.

Transfer cooled sauce to a blender and purée until almost smooth. Season with salt and pepper; set aside. Sauce can be made earlier in the day.

For the salmon, finely grind pecans, tarragon and basil. Blend in butter and season to taste. Transfer mixture to a bowl and cover. Chill.

Preheat oven to 350 degrees.

Arrange salmon on a greased baking pan. Season with salt and pepper and spread pecan mixture over the top. Bake about 20 minutes.

Meanwhile, bring sauce to simmer. Using a spatula, transfer salmon portions to a plate. Spoon sauce around salmon.

Poached Salmon with Mayonnaise

Perfect on a warm, balmy evening. Perhaps with a little champagne, candlelight, soft music and best friends!

3 (8-ounce) bottles clam juice

¾ cup dry white wine

3 lemon slices, plus extra for garnish

3 fresh dill sprigs, plus extra for garnish

4 whole peppercorns

4 (6- to 8-ounce) wild salmon fillets (or one whole half fillet)

Butter lettuce

Tomato wedges for garnish

Mayonnaise (recipe below)

Combine clam juice, white wine, lemon slices, dill sprigs and peppercorns in deep skillet. Simmer 10 minutes.

Add salmon gently. Cover and simmer about 9 minutes per inch.

Transfer to a plate using 2 spatulas; reserving poaching liquid. Serve salmon warm, or cover until chilled and serve cold.

To serve, transfer to a platter lined with butter lettuce and garnished with lemon slices, tomato wedges and fresh dill. Serve with homemade mayonnaise.

MAYONNAISE

1 cup mayonnaise

2 tablespoons lemon juice

2 teaspoons lemon zest

2 tablespoons chopped fresh chives

2 tablespoons chopped fresh parsley

1 tablespoon reserved poaching liquid, or more for desired consistency

Salt and pepper to taste

Combine all ingredients.

Prawns with Saffron Sauce

SERVES 4

It is difficult not to speak in superlatives about this dish – it is absolutely delicious!

16 prawns, the largest available

5 tablespoons unsalted butter, divided

1 shallot, finely chopped

¼ cup cognac or brandy

½ cup Chardonnay wine

1 cup heavy cream

3 pinches of saffron

Dash of Tabasco sauce

Peel and devein prawns, reserving shells.

Melt 2 tablespoons butter in a saucepan. Add reserved prawn shells and shallots and sauté until shells turn pink and shallots are limp. Pour cognac over the shells and shallots and carefully ignite with a match. Remove from heat. When flames die down, return pan to the burner. Add wine and cook over medium heat until reduced to 3 tablespoons.

Strain sauce into a small bowl, pressing hard on the shells to extract all liquid. Return the sauce to the saucepan. Add cream, saffron and Tabasco. Over medium-high heat, reduce sauce until it coats the back of a spoon. Whisk in 2 tablespoons butter; keep warm. There is just enough sauce for four servings – guard carefully!

In a skillet, melt remaining tablespoon of butter. Add prawns and sauté 3 minutes or until they curl slightly and turn pink.

To serve, spoon a pool of sauce onto each serving plate. Arrange prawns on sauce and serve at once.

Since this is a main course, the beauty of the dish is the extra large size of the prawns.

Salmon with Pineapple and Soy

SERVES 8 OR MORE

My friend Ave is fabulous in every way but when she served this and then generously shared the recipe, our admiration went way over the top! You will agree.

1 (46-ounce) can unsweetened
   pineapple juice
¼ cup soy sauce
8 center cut salmon fillets, with
   skin
Sesame seeds

Boil pineapple juice over high heat for 20 minutes or until reduced to 3 cups. Allow to cool completely. Stir in soy sauce.

Cut each salmon fillet in half lengthwise, resulting in sixteen ½-inch thick slices. Marinate salmon in pineapple juice mixture in the refrigerator for up to 3 hours, but no longer.

Preheat oven to 450 degrees. Spray baking pan with nonstick spray.

Remove fish from marinade, reserving marinade. Place fish, skin-side down, on prepared baking pan and cover with foil.

Bake 10 to 15 minutes or until just cooked through. Cool to room temperature. Salmon can be completed the day before and refrigerated. Remove from refrigerator 30 minutes before serving.

Meanwhile, simmer the reserved marinade until thickened slightly. Set aside.

To serve, place field greens mixed with a mild wine vinaigrette on individual plates. Top with salmon. Nap with reduced sauce and sprinkle with sesame seeds.

Absolutely superb!

Shrimp Curry Malaya

SERVES 8

Stop! No need to look any further – this is the definitive Shrimp Curry. The sauce can be made the day before, finishing touches take a few minutes and voilá – elegant company fare!

1 stick butter

2 cloves garlic, minced

1 onion, finely chopped

3 stalks celery, chopped

1 red bell pepper, chopped

1 carrot, finely chopped

1 green apple, peeled and chopped

1 (14-ounce) can petite diced tomatoes

1 tablespoon finely chopped fresh parsley

1 bay leaf

Pinch of dried thyme

Pinch of dried oregano

Pinch of dried marjoram

1 teaspoon dried basil

2 tablespoons flour

3 tablespoons curry powder

Salt and pepper to taste

¼ teaspoon cayenne pepper

Pinch of nutmeg

½ teaspoon cardamom

½ teaspoon turmeric

½ teaspoon mace

2 cups chicken broth

1 cup dry white wine

2 pounds large prawns, peeled and deveined

1 cup heavy cream

Melt butter in large saucepan. Add garlic, onion, celery, bell pepper, carrot, apple, tomatoes, parsley, bay leaf, thyme, oregano, marjoram and basil. Cook until vegetables are soft. Remove the bay leaf.

Mix the flour with curry powder, salt and pepper, cayenne, nutmeg, cardamom, turmeric and mace. Add mixture to cooked vegetables and blend well. Continue to cook 5 minutes, stirring often. Add broth and continue to cook until mixture begins to thicken. Add wine. Cover and cook over low heat for 30 minutes, stirring occasionally.

(Suggest preparing to this point and refrigerating – the flavors improve markedly. Heat sauce gently and proceed with recipe.)

Add prawns and cream to sauce and cook just until prawns turn pink.

Serve immediately with plain or curried rice and sambals.

I like to place sambals in individual small dishes and set one in front of each guest's plate, which are then passed around.

SHRIMP CURRY MALAYA — CONTINUED

SOME OF OUR FAVORITE SAMBALS:
Chopped peanuts or cashews
Grated coconut, plain or toasted
Chopped green onion
Chopped sweet pickle
Chopped hard-boiled egg yolks
Chopped hard-boiled egg whites
Raisins
Currents
Mango chutney
Chopped bananas
Chopped oranges
Chopped papaya
Kumquats
Chopped avocado
Chopped red bell pepper
Watermelon pickle

Seafood Marinade

Use for salmon, swordfish and halibut.

½ **cup soy sauce**
½ **cup olive oil**
Black pepper to taste
Crushed garlic
Juice of 1 lime

Combine all ingredients. Marinade fish of choice in marinade mixture for 1 hour. Remove fish, pat dry and barbecue or broil.

Sizzling Shrimp with Garlic

Hotsy totsy!

4 cloves garlic, minced

½ teaspoon dried red pepper flakes

1 teaspoon sweet paprika

5 tablespoons olive oil

1 pound large prawns, peeled and deveined

2 tablespoons lemon juice

2 tablespoons dry sherry

Salt and pepper to taste

2 tablespoons chopped flat-leaf parsley

Sauté garlic, pepper flakes and paprika in olive oil for 2 minutes over medium heat.

Increase heat and add prawns, lemon juice and sherry. Cook about 3 minutes. Season with salt and pepper and sprinkle with chopped parsley.

Serve with steamed rice, sugar snap peas, Asian beer.

POULTRY

Bammie's Chicken

My darling grandchildren's favorite and most often requested.

8 boneless, skinless chicken
  breasts
Salt and pepper to taste
1 stick butter, melted
3 cloves garlic, minced
2 cups dry seasoned bread crumbs

Preheat oven to 425 degrees.

Flatten chicken breasts between 2 sheets of wax paper. Season with salt and pepper.

Combine butter and garlic in a bowl. Place bread crumbs on a sheet of wax paper.

Dip chicken in butter mixture, then dredge in bread crumbs. Place coated chicken on a baking sheet greased with olive oil.

Bake 10 minutes. Reduce oven to 350 degrees and cook 10 minutes longer.

I can sometime find "thin cut" chicken breasts. These are great.

I use this same recipe for boneless, skinless chicken thighs, increasing the cooking time by 10 minutes. A nice touch when cooking the thighs, after oven temperature is reduced, is to add ½ cup sweet vermouth and continue cooking.

The Best Damn Duck

Robert named this dish, appropriately – I had played around with cooking duck before, but none could measure up to this dish. Topping it off with "The Best Damn Rice" earned me the title Queen for the Day (Night)!

1 (3- to 4-pound) duck, washed and dried

1 lemon

Salt and pepper to taste

½ cup dry sherry

½ cup soy sauce

¼ cup molasses or Chinese bean molasses

1 clove garlic, minced

Preheat oven to 450 degrees

Poke the duck all over with a fork to allow fat to escape. Rub inside with lemon and season all over with salt and pepper. Place duck on a rack in a roasting pan, breast-side up. Bake 15 minutes.

Meanwhile, combine sherry, soy sauce, molasses and garlic in a saucepan and simmer 10 minutes.

Reduce oven to 350 degrees. Cook duck an additional 1 hour, 30 minutes, brushing duck with sherry sauce every 15 minutes and turning duck each time.

THE BEST DAMN RICE

1 duck liver, chopped

1 teaspoon oil

4 ounces sliced mushrooms

1 egg, slightly beaten

2 cups leftover rice (which has been cooked with butter and ½ package onion soup mix)

Sauté liver in oil. Add mushrooms and cook until golden. Add egg and mix quickly with a wooden fork. Add rice and cook until heated through.

Chicken Breasts in Chutney Cream

SERVES 4

This dish is a treat – although it takes very little time to prepare, the result is very special!

4 whole boneless, skinless chicken breasts, split into 8 pieces

⅓ cup flour

6 tablespoons butter, or as needed

2 green onions, finely chopped

½ tablespoon minced fresh ginger

3 tablespoons Major Grey's chutney

⅔ cup Madeira wine

¾ cup chicken broth

¾ cup heavy cream

2 tablespoons chopped crystallized ginger

Curried Rice (page 199)

Parsley sprigs for garnish

Pound chicken breasts to ¼-inch thickness. Dust with flour. Sauté chicken in 3 tablespoons butter in a skillet for 4 to 6 minutes or until golden on both sides. Add more butter as needed. Transfer chicken to a platter.

Add green onions, fresh ginger, chutney, Madeira and broth to skillet. Boil on high until mixture reduces by half. Add cream and reduce to 1¼ cups.

Pour cream sauce over chicken. Sprinkle crystallized ginger on top. Spoon Curried Rice along side. Garnish with parsley.

Chicken Breasts Stuffed with Spinach

MAKES 12 BUNDLES

An old favorite! A very showy buffet dish.

1 medium onion, finely chopped

1 tablespoon butter

1 (10-ounce) package frozen, chopped spinach, thawed and drained dry

1 pound ricotta cheese

1 egg, lightly beaten

¼ cup chopped fresh parsley

1 tablespoon mixed herbs, such as oregano, savory, chervil and marjoram

Salt and pepper to taste

12 boneless chicken breasts with skin

Garlic powder

Preheat oven to 350 degrees.

Sauté onion in butter until soft. Combine onion with spinach, ricotta cheese, egg, parsley and herbs. Season generously with salt and pepper.

Loosen skin of chicken breast. Stuff each breast with ¼ cup of ricotta filling under the skin. Tuck the skin under the meat forming an even, dome shape. Place breasts in a glass baking dish. Sprinkle with salt and pepper and garlic powder.

Bake about 40 minutes; do not overcook.

Serve whole or, for a tasty buffet dish, cool the bundles and then carefully slice, keeping shape intact. Placing on a serving plate, decorating with greens and cherry tomatoes.

Chicken Quinn

Some kids lovingly speak of Mom's Apple Pie, others – Mom's Fried Chicken, but for Quinn – this is IT!

6 tablespoons flour
½ teaspoon salt
¼ teaspoon black pepper
4 large boneless, skinless chicken breasts, slightly flattened
2 eggs
¼ cup milk
3 tablespoons sesame seeds
Canola oil

SAUCE
3 tablespoons butter
2 tablespoons flour
2½ cups chicken broth
Pinch of nutmeg
Salt and pepper to taste
½ cup heavy cream

Combine flour, salt and pepper in a plastic bag. Dredge chicken in seasoned flour. Shake off excess flour.

Beat eggs with milk. Mix in remaining seasoned flour from plastic bag.

Dip chicken in egg mixture and coat with sesame seeds.

Heat oil in a skillet. Fry chicken in oil until golden on both sides. Drain on paper towels and keep warm.

For the sauce, melt butter. Mix in flour and cook and stir for several minutes. Add broth, nutmeg and salt and pepper. Add cream and blend well. Cook until slightly thickened.

Serve chicken with sauce and steamed rice.

Chicken Rustica

A recipe from Bill Dunbar verbatim via e-mail and just before going to press – absolutely fabulous!

THE BROTH

Cook a lot of chicken legs and thighs in the oven with carrots, celery and a couple onions. Salt and pepper, too. Cook the chicken THOROUGHLY until it's quite brown and the juices on the bottom of the pan begin to caramelize.

Despite being a delicious meal in its own right, into a stock pot go all the pan's contents. Be sure to scrape all the dark caramelized bits into the pot, as well.

Add a bunch of peppercorns to the water, a good bit of salt and boil away. It'll take a while to get the broth rich and brown. Not yellow, not beige, not taupe. Brown. Real brown. When it's done, strain it pretty well – but a few small bits of detritus are OK.

It should taste like a soup. Got it?

Now, make risotto with it.

THE CHICKEN

Place whatever parts that float your boat into a large baking pan. Coat the skin with salt, pepper, paprika (don't skimp here!) and a touch of cayenne. Scatter the slices of a couple large sweet onions around the chicken. A bunch of peeled cloves of garlic would be good, too. Maybe twenty.

Cook the chicken for 20-25 minutes at 400 degrees, then add about three cups of sweet vermouth. Cook 20 minutes longer or until done You're looking for a dark brown skin with little hints of orange from the paprika. The onions ought to be flimsy and brown.

Save the pan drippings, removing the fat.

THE PRESENTATION

You have now cooked the best pure risotto of your life. Rejoice. (See Risotto 101, page 205, using this chicken broth recipe.)

CHICKEN RUSTICA — CONTINUED

Dump the risotto into a large serving dish. Place the chicken parts around the perimeter of the risotto. Scatter the cooked onions about the edges, too. Drizzle about ½ cup of the pan sauce over the risotto, then sprinkle Parmigiano-Reggiano cheese on top.

It's fun to serve family-style, with a little gravy boat of pan sauce available for all who want it. The sweetness from the vermouth is a different little element to the normal risotto and chicken route, so don't be bashful.

Mangia!

Chicken Olé

A full-flavored chicken dish. The tamales disintegrate, creating a zesty, creamy sauce over the chicken.

8 chicken breasts, boned, skinned and rolled	Preheat oven to 350 degrees
4 frozen beef tamales, cut in half	In a glass 9x13-inch baking dish, alternate chicken rolls and tamales checkerboard fashion.
1 (10¾-ounce) can condensed cream of chicken soup	
1 cup half-and-half	Mix soup and half-and-half. Pour mixture over chicken and tamales. Sprinkle with cheese and top with olives.
1 cup grated Cheddar cheese	
1 (2¼-ounce) can sliced black olives	
	Cover dish with foil. Bake 30 minutes. Remove foil and bake 30 minutes longer.

Chicken Thighs with Mushrooms

I refer to this chicken recipe as "Faux Veal" – transforms simple thighs to very special.

6 boneless, skinless chicken thighs

Juice of 2 lemons

Salt and pepper to taste

Roasted Garlic Purée (recipe below)

1 cup dried bread crumbs

3 tablespoons grated Parmesan cheese

8 ounces sliced mushrooms

1 tablespoon butter

½ cup heavy cream

Marinate thighs in lemon juice 1 hour. Remove and pat dry. Sprinkle with salt and pepper. Brush both sides with small amount of garlic purée.

Preheat oven to 400 degrees.

Combine bread crumbs and Parmesan cheese. Dip thighs in bread crumb mixture. Place thighs on a baking sheet which has been brushed with olive oil. Bake 30 minutes.

Meanwhile, sauté mushrooms slowly in butter. When golden brown, add cream and cook about 10 minutes.

Remove chicken from oven and top with mushroom mixture.

ROASTED GARLIC PURÉE

4 heads garlic

Olive oil

Slice top off garlic heads. Brush with a generous amount of olive oil. Wrap in foil. Bake at 300 degrees for 35 minutes or until soft. Press out cloves and mash to a purée.

Mix in a little more olive oil. Refrigerate any leftover purée or use for Garlic Baked Potatoes.

CHICKEN THIGHS WITH MUSHROOMS — CONTINUED

GARLIC BAKED POTATOES

2 large potatoes, peeled, cut into large slices

Roasted Garlic Purée

Salt and pepper to taste

Spread garlic purée down each slice and reassemble potatoes. Sprinkle with salt and pepper and wrap in each potato in foil. Bake at 475 degrees for 1 hour or until done. Yummy!

Chicken with Port Mushroom Sauce

SERVES 4

This is absolutely one of my favorite chicken breast recipes. It is elegant, quick to prepare and can easily become another of your signature dishes.

4 tablespoons butter, divided

2 cups sliced mushrooms

4 boneless, skinless chicken breasts

Salt and pepper to taste

1-2 tablespoons flour

1 clove garlic, minced

½ cup tawny port

½ cup chicken broth

½ cup heavy cream

¾ teaspoon coarsely chopped dried rosemary

Melt 2 tablespoons butter in a skillet. Add mushrooms and sauté until golden brown; set mushrooms aside.

Melt remaining 2 tablespoons butter in same pan. Season chicken with salt and pepper and coat with flour, shaking off excess. Sauté chicken in butter for 4 minutes on each side. Transfer to a plate and tent with foil.

Add garlic to skillet and cook 30 seconds. Add port and bring to a boil. Add broth, cream and rosemary and cook until slightly thickened. Return mushrooms to skillet and heat 2 minutes.

To serve, slice chicken on the diagonal and top with mushroom sauce.

Chicken with Walnuts and Plum Sauce

A weekday Chinese feast consisting of store-bought pot stickers, fried eggplant with garlic and onions, sautéed shredded Brussels sprouts with garlic and ginger, sticky rice, chicken with walnuts and plum sauce and orange sherbet. We voted this dinner a winner!

Boiling water

1 cup walnut halves

½ cup plus 1 tablespoon peanut oil, divided

6 boneless, skinless chicken thighs, cut into ½-inch pieces

1 tablespoon beaten egg

1 teaspoon cornstarch

2 green onions, chopped, for garnish

PLUM SAUCE

2 tablespoons plum or hoisin sauce

1 tablespoon chopped fresh ginger

1 teaspoon sugar

1 teaspoon soy sauce

¼ teaspoon sesame oil

Pour boiling water over walnut halves and let stand 5 minutes. Drain and set aside.

When ready to cook, heat ½ cup peanut oil in a wok. Add walnuts and stir-fry 45 seconds or until golden. Remove walnuts from wok and drain on paper towels; reserve oil in wok.

Combine chicken, egg, cornstarch and remaining 1 tablespoon peanut oil. Add to hot oil in wok and cook 3 minutes or until golden. Drain well and set aside. Pour off all but a film of oil.

Mix all sauce ingredients and stir until well combined. Simmer sauce in wok for 1 to 2 minutes. Add chicken and walnuts to sauce and mix thoroughly. Transfer to a serving plate and garnish with green onions. Serve with Eggplant with Garlic and Onions.

CHICKEN WITH WALNUTS AND PLUM SAUCE — CONTINUED

EGGPLANT WITH GARLIC AND ONIONS

1 large eggplant, cut into large cubes

Salt

Vegetable oil

1 tablespoon chopped garlic

1 tablespoon chopped fresh ginger

4 green onions, sliced

1 teaspoon sesame oil

¼ teaspoon dried red pepper flakes

Sprinkle eggplant with salt and drain on paper towel for 30 minutes. Sauté eggplant in vegetable oil until golden. Add garlic, ginger, green onions, sesame oil and pepper flakes. Cook 3 to 4 minutes longer.

Chicken Scaloppini

Amy's specialty. She changes it from time to time with different herbs, shallots instead of garlic, but anyway she cooks this, it is delicious.

6 boneless, skinless chicken breasts

Salt and pepper to taste

Flour

2 tablespoons butter

2 tablespoons olive oil

3 cloves garlic, finely chopped

¼ teaspoon dried oregano

¼ teaspoon dried thyme

½ cup white wine

½ cup dry vermouth

½ cup sweet vermouth

Flatten chicken breasts between plastic wrap until quite thin. Sprinkle salt and pepper over chicken and dust with flour, shaking off any excess. Chicken may be left whole or cut into smaller pieces.

Heat butter and oil in a skillet and sauté 30 seconds on each side. Place on a plate and tent with foil.

Add garlic, oregano and thyme to same pan and cook 10 seconds; do not allow garlic to brown. Add wine and all vermouth. Cook and stir until reduced to a glaze.

Return chicken to skillet and coat with sauce. Serve with risotto.

Divine Duck

This recipe came about when a friend gave us two wild ducks, but we have since used domestic birds with equally delicious results

2 duck breasts, skin removed

2 duck legs, skin removed and end bone chopped off

Buttermilk

2 tablespoons vegetable oil

Apricot Sauce (recipe below)

Submerge duck meat in buttermilk for 4 hours in the refrigerator. Drain and pat dry.

Sauté duck in vegetable oil for 4 minutes on each side for the breasts, 3 minutes longer for the legs, or until browned on all sides. Slice each breast on the diagonal and place alongside the leg. Top with Apricot Sauce.

APRICOT SAUCE

1 large shallot, finely chopped

1 tablespoon unsalted butter

½ cup tawny port

1 tablespoon brandy

⅔ cup dried apricots, cut into thin strips

2 tablespoons balsamic or fig vinegar

1 tablespoon unsalted butter, cut into small pieces

Use a wide skillet to facilitate sauce reducing to a beautiful glaze. Sauté shallot in butter, stirring until soft. Add port and brandy and cook until reduced by half, stirring all the while.

Add apricots and vinegar and simmer until sauce forms a glaze. Stir in butter, a piece at a time. Serve warm over duck.

Elegant Chicken Breasts

This was my standard "company fare" when I was very, very young. I not only impressed my guests, I impressed myself!

4 ounces crabmeat

1 cup dry sherry

4 boneless chicken breasts with skin

Salt and pepper to taste

Flour

1 egg white, beaten

Fine bread crumbs

4 tablespoons butter

Tarragon Cream Sauce (recipe below)

Marinate crab in sherry for 30 minutes. Remove crab and squeeze out the sherry. Gently spread the crab between the skin and meat of the chicken breasts. Season with salt and pepper. Tuck skin under to form a neat packet.

Dip chicken in flour, then egg white, then bread crumbs.

Fry chicken in butter, skin-side down, until golden; do not brown the other side. Place chicken in a baking dish, skin-side up. (Chicken can be refrigerated at this point until ready to bake. Allow 5 additional minutes baking time.)

Preheat oven to 350 degrees.

Bake 20 minutes. Spoon Tarragon Cream Sauce over chicken and serve.

TARRAGON CREAM SAUCE

2 tablespoons butter

2 tablespoons flour

Salt and white pepper to taste

½ teaspoon tarragon

1 cup heavy cream

¼ cup dry sherry

Melt butter in saucepan. Gradually blend in flour and cook several minutes. Season with salt and pepper. Add tarragon and mix well. Add cream and cook and stir until sauce thickens. Add sherry and simmer 2 minutes longer.

Garlic Glazed Chicken

Great!

8-10 boneless chicken thighs with
   skin
Salt and pepper to taste
2 tablespoons olive oil
4 tablespoons butter
1 teaspoon dried thyme, or
   4 sprigs fresh
Roasted Garlic Glaze
   (recipe below)

Preheat oven to 375 degrees.

Season chicken with salt and pepper. Heat olive oil in a large ovenproof skillet. Place chicken, skin-side down, in the hot skillet and sear 8 minutes. Remove skillet from heat. Add butter and thyme.

Place skillet in oven and roast 16 minutes. Remove from oven and carefully turn the chicken so skin-side is up. Brush top of chicken with Roasted Garlic Glaze. Roast, skin-side up, for 10 minutes longer or until skin is crisp. Serve with steamed rice or roasted potatoes.

ROASTED GARLIC GLAZE

20 cloves garlic
½ cup plus 2 tablespoons olive oil,
   divided
1 teaspoon salt, divided
½ teaspoon white pepper, divided
2 eggs yolks
2 tablespoons fresh lemon juice

Preheat oven to 325 degrees.

Place garlic on a sheet of foil. Drizzle with 2 tablespoons olive oil and sprinkle with ½ teaspoon of salt and ¼ teaspoon pepper. Form foil into a packet. Roast about 40 minutes or until garlic is cooked through.

Press out roasted cloves and combine with egg yolks, lemon juice, remaining ½ teaspoon salt and remaining ¼ teaspoon pepper in a food processor. Purée on high speed. Add remaining ½ cup olive oil in a slow stream and process until the glaze is thick and smooth.

Transfer to an airtight container and refrigerate until ready to use. The glaze can be made up to 1 day in advance.

Roasted Garlic Glaze is equally delicious over baked halibut or salmon.

Homey Chicken

It's raining cats and dogs, the fire is blazing away, loved ones are at home and this chicken is cooking away in the oven. Life is good.

6 chicken breasts

6 whole chicken legs

½ cup dry vermouth

4 tablespoons butter, cut into pieces

1 teaspoon dried thyme

½ teaspoon salt

½ teaspoon cracked black pepper

1 onion, sliced and separated into rings

2 cups heavy cream

2½ tablespoons flour

Parsley sprigs for garnish

Preheat oven to 375 degrees

Place chicken pieces, skin-side up, in a large roasting pan. Pour vermouth over chicken and dot with butter. Sprinkle with thyme, salt and pepper. Arrange onion rings over chicken.

Bake 1 hour or until done, basting chicken occasionally with drippings. Remove chicken to a warm platter and keep warm.

Skim fat from drippings in pan. In a small bowl, stir cream and flour until smooth. Add cream mixture to the pan drippings, stirring to loosen brown bits from bottom of pan. Cook over medium heat until sauce thickens.

To serve, spoon a little sauce over chicken. Arrange onion rings over chicken and decorate platter with sprigs of parsley. Pass remaining sauce on the side.

Italian Chicken with Spaghetti Bordelaise

The chicken that lands in this dish makes history! The cook who cooks this dish makes history! And I make history for passing it along to you! It is an Emeril recipe.

½ cup kosher salt

½ cup sugar

8 cups cold water

12 chicken thighs with skin (if desired, add a few large chicken breasts with skin or drumsticks)

Sprinkling of cayenne pepper (go lightly on this)

3 tablespoons olive oil

½ cup or more peeled garlic cloves, half of which are coarsely mashed

2 cups white wine or dry vermouth

3 lemons, quartered

1 teaspoon dried oregano

2 teaspoons dried basil

1 bay leaf

½ cup chopped fresh parsley, plus extra for garnish

Make a brine by combining kosher salt, sugar and cold water.

Trim chicken of excess skin or fat. Add chicken to brine making sure chicken is completely submerged. Soak chicken in brine for at least 2 hours. Drain chicken and pat dry.

Preheat oven to 350 degrees.

Sprinkle chicken very lightly with cayenne. Brown chicken in olive oil in a large paella pan. Remove chicken from pan and set aside. Add mashed garlic to same pan and cook 1 minute. Stir well. Remove pan from heat and add remaining garlic cloves, wine, lemon quarters, oregano, basil, bay leaf and ½ cup parsley. Stir well. Add chicken and cover pan tightly with foil or a cover.

Bake 1 hour. Uncover and roast 30 minutes longer. The sauce is reduced to a nice glaze.

Arrange chicken and sauce over Spaghetti Bordelaise (a must!). Garnish with extra parsley.

ITALIAN CHICKEN WITH SPAGHETTI BORDELAISE — CONTINUED

SPAGHETTI BORDELAISE

½ cup green onions, chopped

½ cup olive oil

8 cloves garlic, minced

2 tablespoons white wine or
   dry vermouth

¾ teaspoon basil

½ teaspoon oregano

½ teaspoon thyme

½ teaspoon salt

⅓ teaspoon freshly ground pepper

3 tablespoons butter

½ cup chopped parsley

1 pound dry spaghetti

1 cup Parmesan cheese

Cook green onions in olive oil for about 2 minutes. Add garlic and mix well. Add wine, basil, oregano, thyme, salt, pepper, butter and parsley and cook 2 minutes.

Cook spaghetti until al dente; drain. Add onion mixture to spaghetti and toss to mix. Place in a large serving bowl. Coat with Parmesan cheese.

Except for cooking spaghetti last minute, Spaghetti Bordelaise can be done several hours ahead.

Mango Chutney Chicken

Everyone wants this recipe!

6 tablespoons butter

2 tablespoons curry powder

¼ cup dry white wine or dry vermouth

2 frying chickens, quartered (or 8 chicken parts with or without skin)

1½ cups mango chutney, chopped with syrup

2 tablespoons shredded coconut, lightly toasted

1 tablespoon chopped chives

Preheat oven to 350 degrees.

Melt butter in a saucepan. Add curry and cook 3 minutes. Add wine and stir until well blended.

Place chicken in a baking pan. Baste with butter mixture.

Bake 30 minutes. Remove from oven and spread chutney over chicken. Bake 30 minutes longer, basting frequently with pan juices.

Remove chicken to a serving platter. Pour pan juices into a small saucepan. Bring to a boil and cook 3 to 4 minutes or until sauce is slightly reduced. Pour sauce over chicken.

Sprinkle with coconut and chives. Serve with rice.

Mexican Mushi

Fun, easy, delicious – great for Monday night football!

¼ **cup soy sauce**

2 **tablespoons cornstarch**

1 **teaspoon grated fresh ginger**

2 **chicken breasts, skinned, boned and thinly slices**

2 **tablespoons vegetable oil**

1 **clove garlic, minced**

Pinch of dried red pepper flakes

½ **(16-ounce) package coleslaw mix**

4 **green onions, thinly sliced**

Black pepper to taste

Flour tortillas

Fresh chives

Plum sauce

Mix together soy sauce, cornstarch and ginger. Add chicken, then shake off any excess.

In a large skillet, heat vegetable oil. Add chicken with garlic and pepper flakes and sauté until chicken is brown. Add coleslaw, green onions and black pepper. Mix well and cook 1 minute.

Heat tortillas. Add several tablespoons of chicken mixture to tortillas, wrap tightly and tie with chives at both ends of tortillas. Serve with plum sauce.

Oven Fried Chicken with Sweet Vermouth

This chicken never goes out of style – easy preparation – easy eating – easy clean-up!

1 **cup Bisquick**

1 **teaspoon salt**

½ **teaspoon black pepper**

2 **teaspoons paprika**

8 **pieces of chicken, with skin**

4 **tablespoons butter, melted**

¾ **cup sweet vermouth**

Preheat oven to 350 degrees.

Combine baking mix, salt, pepper and paprika. Coat chicken with dry mixture. Arrange chicken in a single layer in a baking pan. Pour melted butter over chicken.

Bake, uncovered, for 30 minutes. Add vermouth and bake 15 minutes longer.

Noni's Chicken Curry

Long ago, a nurse in a doctor's office gave me this recipe. I have treasured it ever since. I love it! It is such a great luncheon dish, the book or investment club ladies relish it, the guys gobble it down, and all the while, you remain calm, cool and collected because it takes so little effort to produce such a stunning result. This is truly one of my oldest, most prized recipes.

8 boneless, skinless chicken breasts

Salt and pepper to taste

Sprinkling of garlic powder

1 yellow onion, chopped

1 apple, peeled and chopped

1 stick butter

1-2 tablespoons curry, depending on taste

1 (10¾-ounce) can condensed cream of chicken soup

1 soup can half-and-half or heavy cream

Mango chutney

Topping of choice: Chopped cashews or peanuts, plumped white raisins, sliced green onions, chopped egg whites, chopped egg yolks, diced bananas, diced red pepper, diced sweet pickle, diced watermelon pickle.

Preheat oven to 350 degrees.

Season chicken with salt and pepper and garlic powder. Place in single layer in a baking pan.

Sauté onion and apple in butter until soft. Add curry and continue to cook for several minutes, stirring all the while. Combine soup and cream and add to apple mixture. Pour mixture over chicken.

Bake 1 hour. Serve with steamed rice and top with mango chutney and toppings of choice.

I have used chicken with bones and skin, skinless thighs or with skin and bones – all producing a delicious dish – different but equally good.

Coriander, turmeric, cardamom and other spices can be added to the curry if a spicier, zestier taste is desired.

Pan Roasted Quail with Port Sauce

SERVES 6

Plan to order these ahead AND plan on dazzling your guests!

12 boneless quail

MARINADE
½ **cup red wine**
¼ **cup port**
¼ **cup olive oil, plus extra for**
  sautéing
2 tablespoons balsamic vinegar
2 tablespoons maple syrup
2 tablespoons soy sauce
1 teaspoon dried red pepper
  flakes
2 cloves garlic, minced

WILD RICE STUFFING
(see Wild Rice Salad recipe,
page 69)

PORT SAUCE
1½ **cups port wine**
1 cup brandy
1 (11-oucne) can bouillon soup
1 cup heavy cream

Place quail in a large zip-top bag.

Combine all marinade ingredients and pour over quail. Marinate in refrigerator overnight. Drain quail well and pat dry, discarding marinade.

Preheat oven to 350 degrees.

Stuff quail with Wild Rice Stuffing. Use toothpicks to create neat bundles, tucking in wings and legs. This takes a little patience but produces a professional result.

Sauté quail in olive oil until brown on all sides. Transfer to oven and bake 15 minutes. Remove toothpicks before serving. Serve on a puddle of Port Sauce.

To make sauce, combine wine, brandy and soup in a saucepan. Cook over low heat until sauce reduces to about 1½ cups.

Add cream. Cook over low heat, watching and stirring carefully, until sauce reduces to a glaze.

Phyllo Chicken Packets

Our dear friend, Irene, introduced us to these little bundles. We have each made hundreds of these for various and sundry luncheons and a cast of hundreds have heralded our talent in producing the world's greatest chicken treasures!

¾ cup chopped green onions

¾ cup mayonnaise

1 tablespoon lemon juice

3 cloves garlic, minced, divided

¾ teaspoon dried tarragon

10 tablespoons butter, melted

12 sheets phyllo dough

6 boneless, skinless chicken breast
    halves

Salt and pepper to taste

2 tablespoons Parmesan cheese

Sesame seeds

Mix together green onions, mayonnaise, lemon juice, 2 cloves minced garlic and tarragon; set aside.

Mix remaining garlic clove with melted butter.

For each packet, place 1 sheet of phyllo on a board and brush with 2 teaspoons garlic butter. Arrange a second sheet on top and brush with another 2 teaspoons garlic butter. Lightly sprinkle a chicken breast with salt and pepper and spread 1 side with mayonnaise mixture. Turn over onto phyllo corner and top with more mayonnaise mixture, using about 3 tablespoons of mixture total per chicken breast. Fold over phyllo sides and wrap into a packet.

Place phyllo packets slightly apart on an ungreased baking pan. Brush with remaining garlic butter and sprinkle with Parmesan cheese. At this point, packets can be refrigerated until ready to bake.

Preheat oven to 375 degrees.

Bake 20 to 25 minutes or until golden. Serve hot with a leafy green salad tossed with fresh pears or other fresh fruit.

Tequila Chicken

Have all ingredients assembled when you start cooking and this dish will be ready in minutes!

6 boneless, skinless chicken breasts
Salt and pepper to taste
3 tablespoons butter, divided
1 tablespoon olive oil
1 cup tequila
1 tablespoon lemon juice
1 tablespoon chopped fresh rosemary, or ½ teaspoon dried
1 clove garlic, finely minced
Rosemary sprigs for garnish

Season chicken with salt and pepper. In a large skillet, melt 1 tablespoon butter with olive oil. Add chicken to skillet and sauté 2 minutes or until slightly golden on each side.

Add tequila, lemon juice, rosemary and garlic. Cover and simmer 5 minutes or until the chicken is no longer pink in the center.

Remove chicken to a serving plate; keep warm. Return skillet to burner and increase heat. Cut remaining 2 tablespoons butter into small pieces. Add butter, piece by piece, until sauce is thickened slightly.

Serve chicken with sauce and decorate with springs of rosemary.

Yum! Yum! Drums

1 stick butter, melted

1½ tablespoons Dijon mustard

1½ cups panko bread crumbs

½ cup Parmesan cheese

2 tablespoons chopped fresh
  parsley

2 teaspoons onion powder

1 teaspoon paprika

1 teaspoon dried thyme

1 teaspoon salt

¼ teaspoon black pepper

12 chicken drumsticks, end of
  bone chopped off

SAUCE

1 cup heavy cream

1 clove garlic, minced

Reserved butter/mustard mixture

Preheat oven to 350 degrees.

Combine butter and mustard in a shallow dish. In a separate dish, mix bread crumbs with Parmesan cheese, parsley, onion powder, paprika, thyme, salt and pepper. Roll drumsticks in butter mixture, then roll in crumbs, reserving any leftover butter mixture. Arrange drumsticks on a greased baking sheet.

Bake 30 minutes. Turn gently and bake 30 minutes longer.

Meanwhile, prepare sauce. Cook cream until slightly thickened. Add garlic and butter mixture.

Serve chicken warm or at room temperature. To serve, place a puddle of sauce on a plate and top with drumsticks. Sooo-o-o-o good!

Beef Ribs with Super Sauce

A Tahoe creation – snowing, cozy fires, food, wine, fun! This is a great dinner.

6 beef ribs with bones
1 large yellow onion, sliced
Crazy Jane salt and pepper
Water to cover

SUPER SAUCE
1 cup catsup
¼ cup soy sauce
½ cup seasoned rice vinegar
1 tablespoon brown sugar
½ teaspoon dry mustard
¼ cup water
Pinch red pepper flakes
2 green onions, finely sliced
6 cloves garlic, chopped

VEGETABLE SOUP BONUS
1 (1-ounce) package dry onion
**   soup mix**
1 yellow onion, chopped
⅓ cabbage, shredded
3 large carrots, sliced
12 green beans, 1-inch pieces
2 zucchini, sliced
½ cup dry barley
½ (10-ounce) package frozen
**   petite peas**

Place beef ribs and onion in a large pot. Season with Crazy Jane salt and pepper. Add enough water to cover meat and cook 2 hours or until beef is tender. Transfer meat only to a baking dish just large enough to fit ribs in a single layer. Reserve broth in pot.

Preheat oven to 350 degrees.

Combine all sauce ingredients. Top ribs with sauce and cover dish with foil. Bake 45 minutes.

And now, for the Vegetable Soup Bonus. To reserved broth in pot, add onion soup mix, onion, cabbage, carrot, green beans, zucchini and barley. Cook until tender. Add peas and cook 1 minute. Serve with Parmesan cheese.

Beef Short Ribs with Farfalle Pasta

What could be easier for a stunning result!

4 beef short ribs (ask butcher to cut from the prime rib)

1 (11-ounce) can bouillon soup

½ soup can red wine

Farfalle pasta, cooked al dente and drained

Preheat oven to 350 degrees.

Pack short ribs tightly into a tightly covered casserole dish. (I love my LeCreuset small oblong casserole.) Add bouillon and wine.

Bake 2 hours. Remove from oven and allow to stand several hours.

When ready to serve, reheat and serve over drained farfalle pasta.

Chili Con Carne for a Crowd

SERVES 12-14

Grated Cheddar cheese, a sprinkling of chopped red onion, a dollop of sour cream, a roaring fire, red wine, a thunderstorm and loved ones! Heaven!

4 pounds lean ground beef

6 onions, chopped

2 red bell peppers, chopped

6 cloves garlic, chopped

4 (28-ounce) cans diced tomatoes

3 tablespoons chili powder

1 teaspoon cumin

2 tablespoons dried oregano

2 tablespoons dried basil

Salt to taste

4 (15-ounce) cans kidney beans, drained

Saute beef until brown. Add onion and bell peppers and sauté until soft. Add garlic, tomatoes, chili powder, cumin, oregano, basil and salt. Simmer 1½ hours.

Add kidney beans and cook until heated through.

Chili is better made the day ahead.

Meatloaf with Glamour

That's right – glamour!

1¼ pounds ground beef round

4 slices wheatberry bread, made into crumbs

½ cup chopped dried apricots

2 eggs

2 shallots, finely chopped

2 tablespoons Dijon mustard

1 tablespoon dried sage

1 teaspoon salt

½ teaspoon black pepper

TOPPING

¼ cup apricot preserves

2 tablespoons Dijon mustard

Preheat oven to 425 degrees.

Combine beef, bread crumbs, apricots, eggs, shallots, mustard, sage, salt and pepper. Mix well, using a light hand. Shape mixture into 4 loaves, each about 1-inch thick.

Place loaves on a rimmed baking sheet. Bake 10 minutes.

For topping, mix apricot preserves and mustard and brush generously over loaves. Bake 10 minutes longer.

Serve with whipped buttered yams and buttered green beans.

Oxtail Stew for Sports

SERVES 8

I cannot understand why so many people (my children included) state they do not like Oxtail Stew! This is one of my best, most delicious recipes. Let's form a club for Oxtail Stew Lovers – "The OSL'S"!

6 pounds oxtails

½ teaspoon Crazy Jane salt

3 tablespoons flour

36 whole garlic cloves

20 pitted green olives

2 cups red wine

2 (11-ounce) cans bouillon soup

1 cup port

Zest of 2 oranges, plus extra for garnish

1 tablespoon dried thyme

1 tablespoon dried rosemary

1 teaspoon sage

1 tablespoon chopped fresh Italian parsley, plus extra for garnish

1 tablespoon cornstarch, optional

Preheat oven to 350 degrees.

In the morning, arrange oxtails in a single layer in a large covered casserole dish. Add salt, flour, garlic, olives, red wine, soup, port, orange zest, thyme, rosemary, sage and parsley. Cover casserole first with foil, then with the casserole cover.

Bake 2½ hours or until tender. When done, turn off oven, leaving dish in oven. When cool enough to handle, drain sauce into a large bowl. Place bowl in freezer until fat has solidified; discard fat.

Transfer sauce to a large pan and reduce until slightly thickened. If needed, to thicken sauce, mix cornstarch with cold water and blend into sauce. Return sauce to casserole dish and reheat 30 minutes.

Garnish with additional orange zest and parsley. Serve with mashed potatoes or polenta.

Porcupines

SERVES 4

It is a wonder my children haven't grown quills! Every time we went out and left them it was either macaroni and cheese or porcupines! They still love them!

1 (15-ounce) can tomato sauce, or
   1 (10¾-ounce) can condensed
   tomato soup

2 cups water

1 bay leaf

1 pound lean ground beef

¼ cup dehydrated chopped onion

½ cup dry rice

½ teaspoon salt

¼ teaspoon black pepper

1 teaspoon dried basil

1 teaspoon dried parsley

4 carrots, sliced

Combine tomato sauce, water and bay leaf in a medium saucepan. Simmer gently.

Mix ground beef, onion, rice, salt, pepper, basil and parsley. Form mixture into medium meatballs. Drop meatballs into simmering tomato sauce.

Add carrots. Cover saucepan and cook over low heat for 15 to 20 minutes.

Shortribs – Plain and Simple

Some of the simplest things in life are best!

8 short ribs with bones
1 large onion, quartered
20 cloves garlic
4 carrots, sliced
2 stalks celery, sliced
1 (1-ounce) package dry onion
soup mix
2 cups water
Salt and pepper to taste

Preheat oven to 400 degrees.

Place ribs and onion in a baking pan. Brown in oven for 30 minutes. Reduce heat to 350 degrees.

Transfer ribs and onion to a covered casserole dish. Add garlic, carrot, celery, soup mix, water and salt and pepper. Cover tightly. Bake 2 hours. Turn off oven and leave casserole dish in oven until cool.

Strain all liquid from casserole into a bowl. Place bowl in freezer until fat has congealed; remove fat and discard.

Add sauce to meat in casserole dish. Heat until bubbly.

Spanish Tripe

No one in my family likes tripe. I love it! And I have sophisticated, intelligent friends who like it – so, there! This is for us.

3 pounds honeycomb tripe

1 teaspoon salt

1 large onion, chopped

2 tablespoons canola oil

3 tablespoons parsley, chopped

1 teaspoon dried rosemary

3 cloves garlic, finely chopped

1 (8-ounce) can tomato sauce

1 (14½-ounce) can whole
   tomatoes, coarsely chopped

1 cup chopped celery

6 carrots, cut into large pieces

4 potatoes, cut into large pieces

Wash the tripe under cold running water several times. Cut into 2-inch pieces. Place in a large pot and bring to a boil; drain and rinse. Fill pot again with water and bring to a boil. Add salt and cook tripe 1 hour or until tender. Drain and rinse.

Sauté onion in oil until just soft. Add parsley, rosemary, garlic and tomato sauce. Simmer 30 minutes. Add tripe and cook 30 minutes longer or until tripe is tender.

Add tomatoes, celery, carrot and potato and simmer until tender.

Wonderful over soft polenta!

Steak au Poivre

SERVES 4

Ta Da! Here it is! The steak that makes anyone who serves this – famous! It is the best company dish ever! Marilyn first served this to us many, many years ago. The multitude thanks her!

Crazy Jane pepper

4 (1¾-inch thick) filet mignon steaks, trimmed of all fat

1 cup red wine

1 cup cognac or brandy

1 (11-ounce) can bouillon soup

1 cup heavy cream

Sprigs of fresh parsley or rosemary for garnish

Press pepper onto both sides of steak, flattening steak with the heel of your hand; set aside.

Combine wine, cognac and bouillon in a large skillet. Cook over medium heat, stirring often, until reduced to 1½ cups. This will take quite a while, check often.

Add cream and continue to cook until reduced to the consistency of thick melted chocolate! Set aside. The sauce takes time but the slow cooking is necessary for the proper result. Sauce can be made early in the day and reheated. Sauce recipe can be doubled if needed.

Heat a non stick skillet. Brown steaks nicely on both sides without using fat or oil; do not overcook – meat must be rare. Remove steaks from pan and tent with foil to keep warm.

To serve, reheat sauce. Place steaks in sauce, turning quickly to mask both sides with sauce. Do not cook – it is not a steak and gravy presentation. Can also be served by placing several spoonfuls of sauce on plate and setting the steak atop.

Decorate with parsley or rosemary. Best served with Accordion Potatoes (page 159).

Steak for All Seasons

Whether it is the Fourth of July or snow is on the ground, there are times when a really good piece of red meat is craved! The flavor of this sauce enhances every morsel – be sure to have French bread to sop up every drop.

½ cup olive oil

½ cup soy sauce

¼ cup balsamic vinegar

8 cloves garlic, minced

4 teaspoons dried rosemary, crumbled

4 New York steaks

Salt and pepper to taste

Combine olive oil, soy sauce, vinegar, garlic and rosemary in a glass baking dish. Add steaks and turn to coat. Season with salt and pepper. Cover dish and refrigerate at least 4 hours or overnight.

Before cooking, bring steaks to room temperature. Remove steaks from marinade and pat dry; set aside. Pour marinade into a small saucepan. Bring to a boil; watching carefully. Remove from heat.

Broil steaks at least 5 minutes on each side. Serve sauce over steaks.

The Best Swedish Meatballs

I should charge for this recipe!

1 cup bread crumbs

1⅓ cups milk

1 egg

1 pound lean ground beef

1 teaspoon salt

⅛ teaspoon black pepper

¼ teaspoon nutmeg

2 tablespoons butter

2 tablespoons flour

1½ cups canned bouillon soup

⅓ cup heavy cream or half-and-half

Soak bread crumbs in milk. Gently mix in egg, beef, salt, pepper and nutmeg. Form mixture into small meatballs.

Brown meatballs in butter in a saucepan. Remove meatballs and blend flour into pan drippings. Gradually mix in bouillon and cream. Stir well.

Return meatballs to saucepan and bring to a simmer. Cook 15 minutes. Serve with rice or mashed potatoes.

Tamale Pie

This is a difficult recipe to spell out – it is different every time that I throw it together and we love it any which way! It is always a part of our New Year's Day Open House buffet where it is not unusual to have between 50 and 75 friends. Therefore, the following ingredients are multiplied accordingly. Peek at this all-fattening menu!

WHOLE BAKED HAM WITH
FRUITED MUSTARD SAUCE À LA ROBERT

BAKERY ROLLS

TAMALE PIE

SWEET PICKLES AND RELISHES

MY POTATO SALAD

FRUIT SALAD

CHEESES

LENTIL SOUP
(GOOD LUCK FOR THE NEW YEAR!)

CHAMPAGNE PUNCH AND WINE

ASSORTED COOKIES AND CANDIES

TAMALE PIE — CONTINUED

AND NOW — THE RECIPE...

2 pounds lean ground beef

1 large onion, chopped

2 tablespoons oil

4 cloves garlic, chopped

1 (1-ounce) package enchilada or taco mix

3 tablespoons chili powder

1 red bell pepper, chopped

1 (16-ounce) can corn

1 (28-ounce) can chopped tomatoes

1 (4-ounce) can chopped green chiles

1 (5-ounce) can pitted olives, chopped

1 cup cornmeal

1 cup shredded Monterey Jack cheese

1 cup shredded Cheddar cheese

Corn chips

Preheat oven to 350 degrees.

Cook beef until browned; set aside. Add onion and sauté in oil until soft. Mix in garlic, enchilada mix, chili powder, bell pepper, corn, tomatoes, chiles and olives. Blend in cornmeal.

Spoon mixture into a 9x13-inch glass baking dish. Top with both cheeses.

Bake 50 minutes. Arrange corn chips around the edges of baking dish. Bake 10 minutes longer.

Beer Ribs

These ribs are a hit with both beer drinkers and non-beer drinkers – succulent morsels! A little potato salad, some coleslaw, a cold bottle of something, and you are in Heaven!

4 pounds baby back ribs, halved crosswise and then cut into 1-inch sections by butcher

½ (12-ounce) bottle dark beer

½ cup soy sauce

⅓ cup Dijon mustard

⅔ cup dark brown sugar

1 onion, finely chopped

1 tablespoon Worcestershire sauce

Combine all ingredients in a large plastic zip-top bag. Marinate ribs in refrigerator for 6 hours or overnight.

When ready to cook, preheat oven to 350 degrees.

Drain ribs and place in a large, foil-lined baking pan; reserve marinade. Bake ribs 1 hour, brushing occasionally with marinade.

Brine

This is a good master recipe for brining a pork roast. An extra large plastic bag seems to work best.

2½ gallons cold water

2 cups kosher salt

½ cup sugar

2 bay leaves

¼ cup dried thyme

1 whole head garlic, peeled

Combine all ingredients in a saucepan and bring to a boil. Cool completely.

Submerge a pork roast in brine and refrigerate overnight. Remove from brine and pat roast dry.

Proceed with favorite recipe.

Braised Pork with Apples

On a cold winter's night.

3 pounds boneless pork shoulder, cut into 1-inch cubes

Salt and pepper to taste

Olive oil

1 onion, sliced

4 cloves garlic, sliced

2 shallots, sliced

1 cup plus 1 tablespoon hard cider, divided

½ cup white wine

½ apple, finely chopped

1 tablespoon dried thyme

½ cup heavy cream

1 tablespoon butter

1 apple, peeled and sliced

3 green onions, sliced

Preheat oven to 325 degrees.

Season pork with salt and pepper. Heat olive oil in a large skillet over high heat. In several batches, add pork and brown on all sides. Transfer pork to a Dutch oven or braising pan.

Add onion, garlic and shallots to skillet and sauté until golden. Add 1 cup cider, wine, chopped apple and thyme. Simmer several minutes.

Add mixture to pork. Cover and bake 1 hour or until pork is tender.

Pour pan sauce into a skillet. Add cream and cook to reduce until slightly thickened.

Melt butter in a separate skillet. Add sliced apple and sauté until apple is almost tender. Add green onions and cook until apple is tender.

Return cream sauce to Dutch oven. Add sautéed apples and remaining 1 tablespoon cider. Cover pan and bake at 300 degrees to warm.

Serve with Orzo and Roasted Butternut Squash (page 153).

Crown Roast of Pork with Wild Rice Cranberry Stuffing

Truly special for 12 special guests!

1 crown roast of pork with 18-20 chops, trimmed of fat

Wild Rice Cranberry Stuffing (see page 123)

Spiced apples or kumquats and watercress sprigs for garnish

Wine Sauce (see page 123)

Preheat oven to 350 degrees.

Place pork roast on a rack in a large roasting pan. Place a jar or bowl in the center to avoid collapsing of the chops.

Roast pork 20 minutes per pound. One hour before roast has completed cooking, remove jar or bowl and fill the center of the crown with Wild Rice Cranberry Stuffing, piling it quite high. Continue roasting remaining hour.

Extra stuffing can be put into a greased baking dish, covered and baked 1 hour, then piled in the center of the finished roast for presentation.

Place roast on a platter. Reserve drippings in pan for Wine Sauce.

Garnish roast with apples or kumquats and watercress. Serve with Wine Sauce.

CROWN ROAST OF PORK WITH
WILD RICE CRANBERRY STUFFING — CONTINUED

WILD RICE AND CRANBERRY STUFFING

2 cups dry wild rice

1 (48-ounce) container chicken broth

1 cup raw cranberries, coarsely chopped

4 green onions, chopped

1 tablespoon salt

½ teaspoon marjoram

2 cloves garlic, minced

½ teaspoon black pepper

½ teaspoon mace

½ teaspoon dried thyme

Cook rice in broth in a saucepan until done. Mix in cranberries, green onions, salt, marjoram, garlic, pepper, mace and thyme. Cook over low heat for 15 minutes, stirring often.

Allow to cool. Place in pork roast or in a greased baking dish and cover. Bake at 350 degrees for 1 hour.

WINE SAUCE

¼ cup deglazed pan drippings

¼ cup flour

1 cup dry white wine

½ cup chicken broth

½ heavy cream

Salt and pepper to taste

Blend drippings with flour and cook 3 minutes. Add wine and cook until thickened. Add broth and cream and cook 5 minutes longer. Season with salt and pepper.

Fig-Stuffed Pork Tenderloin

This is truly company fare! There are several steps necessary for this grand achievement, but they are easy steps and can be done ahead. Just delicious!

STUFFING
8 ounces dried Mission figs
3 shallots, chopped
4 cloves garlic, chopped
1 cup Port wine
8 ounces almonds, toasted and chopped

SAUCE
2 cups port wine
¼ cup raspberry vinegar
¼ cup balsamic vinegar
¼ cup brown sugar

BRINE
2 quarts water
⅔ cup kosher salt
⅔ cup brown sugar

MEAT
2 pork tenderloins, brined for 2 to 4 hours
Salt and pepper to taste
4 tablespoons olive oil
Chopped green onions for garnish

Combine all stuffing ingredients in a food processor and process until well blended; set aside. Stuffing can be prepared days ahead.

For the sauce, mix wine, both vinegars and brown sugar in small saucepan. (The "saucier" pan is ideal for this and is worth the investment – useful for reducing all sauces.) Reduce the sauce over low heat until sauce coats the back of a spoon and is a beautiful glaze. Watch the pot carefully towards the end of cooking time. The sauce can be made early in the day and set aside, but do not refrigerate.

To make brine, mix all ingredients in a large saucepan. Bring to a boil. Remove from heat and cool thoroughly.

Soak pork tenderloin in brine for 2 to 4 hours before cooking. Remove pork from liquid and pat dry.

Use a boning knife to cut a slit in the center of the meat. Push finger into slit to widen the hole. Use a pastry bag to pipe stuffing through the hole. Season with salt and pepper.

Preheat oven to 450 degrees.

FIG-STUFFED PORK TENDERLOIN — CONTINUED

Heat olive oil in a pan over medium high heat. Add pork and sauté on all sides. Finish cooking in oven for 8 to 10 minutes. Remove from oven and allow to rest 5 minutes.

Cut pork into thick diagonal slices and place on plates. Drizzle sauce over and around pork. Garnish with chopped green onions.

A knockout dish!

Grilled Marinated Pork Chops

SERVES 6-8

Wow!

1 cup apple juice

¾ cup soy sauce, divided

½ cup honey

2 large garlic cloves, pressed

2 tablespoons grated fresh ginger

2 tablespoons dry mustard

2 dashes Worcestershire sauce

½ cup golden or dark rum

12 (1-inch thick) pork chops

1 (12-ounce) jar apple jelly or apricot jam

3 tablespoons lemon juice

Freshly grated nutmeg to taste

In a bowl, combine apple juice, ½ cup soy sauce, honey, garlic, ginger, mustard, Worcestershire sauce and rum.

Arrange pork chops in a shallow dish in a single layer. Pour marinade over chops and refrigerate overnight, turning occasionally.

Remove chops and set aside. Drain marinade into a saucepan. Add jelly and remaining ¼ cup soy sauce. Bring to a boil and continue cooking until reduced to 1½ cups. Stir in lemon juice and nutmeg.

Grill pork chops on an oiled rack set about inches over glowing coals, turning and basting with the sauce every 5 minutes, for a total of 20 minutes or until just cooked through. Serve chops with remaining sauce.

Grilled Pork Tenderloin with Orange Sauce

Lib's specialty – yum!

½ **cup olive oil**
½ **cup soy sauce**
½ **cup orange juice**
6 **cloves garlic, minced**
2 **teaspoons Dijon mustard**
Black pepper
1 **tablespoon brown sugar**
3 **pork tenderloins**
Sliced oranges and parsley for garnish

Mix together olive oil, soy sauce, orange juice, garlic, mustard, pepper and brown sugar. Add tenderloins. Marinate 3 hours.

Wipe meat dry, reserving marinade. Grill to desired degree of doneness.

In the meantime, reduce the marinade over low heat until syrupy.

Slice tenderloins and cover with sauce. Place on pretty dish and decorate with slices of orange and parsley.

A wild rice casserole is very good with this dish.

Italian Sausage

MAKES 12 POUNDS

Probably the oldest recipe in this collection – our great uncle was famous for these sausages. I can see him now, barbecuing them on the grill out at the beach. A French roll and a glass of red wine and you have created a feast!

12 pounds very coarsely ground pork butt

4 level tablespoons salt

2 level tablespoons black pepper

5 level tablespoons fennel seed

1 cup white wine

Sausage casing for "Italian size sausage" (purchased from your butcher)

Lightly combine all ingredients except casing, being careful not to "mash" the meat.

Rinse casing thoroughly in lemon and water. Attach sausage attachment funnel onto a meat grinder. Thread casing onto the funnel. Omit the blades of the meat grinder as you do not want to regrind the meat.

Feed sausage mixture into funnel to form sausage.

Make these with the family – they freeze beautifully.

Pork Rib Roast with Cider Sauce

One of the best pork dishes.

1 (10-rib) pork loin roast,
  Frenched and trimmed

3 cloves garlic, thinly sliced

Salt and pepper to taste

2 tablespoons coarsely chopped
  fresh thyme

1 tablespoon olive oil

2 medium-size red onions, cut into
  wedges kept intact at the root
  end

4 Bartlett pears, cut into wedges

CIDER SAUCE

1½ quarts pear or apple cider

1 cinnamon stick

1 whole clove

2 thyme sprigs

2 shallots, minced

Thyme leaves

Cherry tomatoes and lemon leaves
  for garnish

Preheat oven to 400 degrees.

Make incisions in roast. Place a slice of garlic in each slit. Season with salt and pepper and sprinkle top of roast with thyme.

Add olive oil to a roasting pan. Set roast in pan and surround with onion wedges. Roast 45 minutes.

Add pears, coating with drippings. Continue roasting 30 minutes or until thermometer registers 160 degrees.

Meanwhile, prepare sauce by combining cider, cinnamon stick, clove and thyme sprigs in a saucepan. Bring to a boil over high heat. Cook 30 minutes or until reduced to 2½ cups.

Arrange pork on large platter. Surround with onions and pears and cover with foil until ready to serve.

Discard fat from roasting pan and set over medium heat. Add shallots and wilt for 3 minutes. Add cider sauce and bring to a boil, scraping up browned bits. Reduce to 1 cup. Strain sauce and add thyme leaves. Serve with sauce on the side.

Garnish with cherry tomatoes and lemon leaves.

Pork Tenderloin with Candied Ginger Purée

This is an excellent buffet dish. Makes delicious sandwiches with small squares of focaccia This is an inexpensive but showy dish.

½ **cup olive oil**

½ **cup soy sauce**

½ **cup orange juice**

6 **cloves garlic, minced**

2 **teaspoons Dijon mustard**

Black pepper to taste

1 **tablespoon brown sugar**

3 **pork tenderloins**

Candied Ginger Purée (see below)

Orange zest and chopped parsley for garnish

Combine olive oil, soy sauce, orange juice, garlic, mustard, pepper and brown sugar. Add pork tenderloins and marinate overnight.

Preheat oven to 400 degrees.

Scrape off and discard marinade. Sauté tenderloins until golden brown on all sides. Transfer to oven and bake about 15 minutes, depending on size – larger tenderloins can be baked a few minutes longer. Do not overcook.

Remove from oven and baste generously with Candied Ginger Purée.

Allow to rest 15 minutes. Cut straight down into slices. Arrange on a serving plate, keeping slices in order of being cut.

Sprinkle with orange zest and decorate platter with parsley.

CANDIED GINGER PURÉE

½ **cup coarsely diced candied ginger**

½ **cup sugar**

1 **cup orange juice**

Combine ginger and sugar in a small food processor until finely crumbled.

Place in a small saucepan and mix in orange juice. Cook until slightly thickened.

Ring-Around-the-Rosy Ham

This is one of my newspaper column recipes from the '60's! It continues to be delicious in this new century! This is so ol'fashioned – so good.

1 large precooked ham
Whole cloves
1 cup brown sugar
¼ cup cornstarch
½ teaspoon ground cloves
¼ teaspoon salt
1 cup orange juice
3 cups cranberry juice
1 cup golden raisins

Preheat oven to 325 degrees.

Bake ham for 15 minutes per pound. Forty minutes before ham is done cooking, remove from oven and discard any fat. Score ham into diagonals, ¼-inch deep. Place a whole clove in each diagonal. Return to oven.

Meanwhile, combine brown sugar, cornstarch, ground cloves, salt, orange juice, cranberry juice and raisins in a saucepan. Cook, stirring constantly, until mixture thickens and comes to a slow boil.

With 20 minutes of baking left, spoon sauce over scored ham. Return to oven and bake 20 minutes longer or until ham is beautifully glazed.

Slice and serve with remaining sauce on the side.

Grilled Pork Chops

This is the way the restaurants achieve succulent pork chops – it's all in the brine. The size of the chops is for the hearty among us!

10 cups water
½ cup kosher salt
⅓ cup sugar
10 thyme sprigs
1 head garlic, halved crosswise
1 tablespoon peppercorns
1 teaspoon dried red pepper flakes
2 oranges, halved crosswise
4 (12-ounce, 1½-inch thick) center cut pork chops

Combine all ingredients except pork chops in a saucepan. Simmer 1 hour. Cool brine completely.

Soak pork chops in brine for 6 to 12 hours. Remove, pat dry and grill.

The size of these chops is important. Can be cut in half if too large for one person but do not use a thinner chop.

Butterflied Leg of Lamb

Everyone should have an Uncle Benny! This is this recipe verbatim. Picture him in the woods behind his Lake Tahoe home, barbecuing the lamb to perfection. And Auntie Stella "guiding" him all the way!

1 leg of lamb, butterflied
Sprigs of fresh rosemary
1 head garlic, crushed
Black pepper
1 cup soy sauce
¾ cup olive oil

Marinate lamb in a mixture of rosemary, garlic, pepper, soy sauce and olive oil for 4 hours.

Barbecue lamb 40 minutes "not too much coal – not too hot".

Traditionally terrific!

Lamb in Yogurt with Almonds

This was our "company" lamb for years. Wonderful flavors.

1 leg of lamb, butterflied
1 cup plain yogurt
1 teaspoon ginger
1 teaspoon chili powder
4 cloves garlic, minced
⅓ cup ground almonds
1 teaspoon salt
1 stick butter, melted

Prick lamb all over with a fork.

In a roasting pan, combine yogurt, ginger, chili powder, garlic, almonds and salt. Add lamb to pan and coat with yogurt marinade. Cover loosely and refrigerate at least 8 hours. Remove and let stand 4 hours at room temperature.

Preheat oven to 350 degrees.

Bake, uncovered, for 15 minutes. Reduce heat to 300 degrees and bake 3 hours, basting frequently. Add butter to the drippings for basting.

Leftovers can be cut into large cubes. Sauté with an onion in butter with a goodly amount of curry powder, a little chicken broth, some cream and you have a superb curry.

Lamb Shanks with Chutney

A treat not to be beat! Prepare early in the day for full flavor.

4 meaty and lean lamb shanks
2 tablespoons oil
1 (14½-ounce) can diced tomatoes
2-3 teaspoons curry powder
1 teaspoon ground ginger
1 (11-ounce) can beef consommé
4 cloves garlic, minced
1 medium onion, finely chopped
½ cup mango chutney

Preheat oven to 350 degrees.

Brown lamb shanks well in oil for 5 minutes in a large heavy skillet. Transfer to a 3-quart Dutch oven.

In a blender, place tomatoes, curry, ginger, consommé, garlic, onion and chutney and blend on low speed until well mixed but not puréed. Pour mixture over lamb shanks.

Cover pan and bake 2 hours. Correct seasoning if necessary.

A dollop of chutney on each shank along with parslied rice makes this a very yummy dish!

Lamb Stew with Calamata Olives

Guests will love this, as will you since it is best made the day before. Deep and rich flavors.

3 pounds lean lamb shoulder or leg meat, cut into small pieces

Salt and pepper to taste

2 tablespoons olive oil

4 shallots, diced

1 large red onion, chopped

6 cloves garlic, finely chopped

1 tablespoon chopped fresh rosemary

1½ cups white wine

1 cup pitted calamata olives

2 tablespoons tomato paste, mixed with ¼ cup water

Preheat oven to 350 degrees.

Season lamb with salt and pepper. Sauté lamb in olive oil in an ovenproof pan in 2 batches until brown. Remove to a plate and keep warm.

In same pan, sauté shallots and onion until golden. Add garlic and rosemary and cook 1 minute.

Return lamb to pan and add wine. Simmer until liquid is reduced by half. Add olives and tomato paste mixed with water and stir thoroughly.

Bake, uncovered, for 1 hour. Can be served immediately, but best if made the day before and refrigerated.

If a thicker sauce is desired, remove the meat and cook until sauce is slightly thickened. Great over polenta or over garlic mashed potatoes.

Leg of Lamb with Olive Paste and Spicy Peanut Sauce

3 tablespoons prepared olive paste

2 teaspoons fresh thyme leaves, or 1 teaspoon dried

1 teaspoon chopped fresh rosemary, or 1 teaspoon dried

Zest of 1 orange

Pinch of kosher salt

1 tablespoon olive oil

3 cloves garlic, minced

1 leg of lamb, butterflied, rolled and tied at 1-inch intervals

Sprigs of fresh rosemary

½ cup white wine

SPICY PEANUT SAUCE

½ cup crunchy peanut butter

2 tablespoons soy sauce

2 cloves garlic, minced

¼ cup chicken broth

2 tablespoons honey

1 tablespoon chili oil

2 tablespoons lemon juice

Combine olive paste, thyme, rosemary, orange zest, salt, olive oil and garlic. Cut deep slashes around the lamb and push ½ teaspoon of mixture into each hole. Refrigerate at least 6 hours.

Remove from refrigerator 1 hour before roasting.

Preheat oven to 450 degrees.

Tuck rosemary sprigs around the roast and sprinkle with additional salt. Roast 10 minutes. Reduce heat to 350 degrees and pour wine over lamb. Roast 20 minutes, basting twice.

Reduce oven temperature to 275 degrees and roast 30 minutes longer, basting periodically. Internal temperature should be 140 degrees for medium rare.

Transfer lamb to a carving board and allow to rest 15 minutes. Slice and serve with Spicy Peanut Sauce.

To make sauce, combine all ingredients and mix well.

Rack of Lamb with Port Sauce

SERVES 6

Nothing could be finer! This is Libbie's method, which produces an excellent result.

½ cup olive oil

½ cup soy sauce

4 cloves garlic, chopped

Sprigs of fresh rosemary, plus extra for garnish

Black pepper to taste

3 racks of lamb

PORT SAUCE

2 (11-ounce) cans beef consommé

2 soup cans brandy

2 soup cans port wine

2 soup cans heavy cream

Combine olive oil, soy sauce, garlic, rosemary and pepper in a large plastic zip-top bag.

Trim all fat from racks of lamb including any fat between bones, creating "Frenched" elongated bones. Cut racks into double chops, yielding 12 pieces.

Add lamb to mixture in plastic bag and marinate in refrigerator for 3 to 4 hours.

Meanwhile, prepare sauce by combining consommé, brandy and port in a large saucepan. Simmer, stirring occasionally, for at least 1 hour or until sauce reduces to a syrup consistency. Add cream and continue to simmer until thickened to a melted chocolate appearance. Sauce can be made ahead and heated before serving. Sauce can be frozen indefinitely.

Remove meat from marinade; reserving marinade. Place lamb on large foil-lined baking sheet. Broil on one side for 5 minutes.

Remove and roll chops in reserved marinade. Remove rosemary. Broil an additional 3 minutes.

To serve, place dollops of sauce on individual plates. Top with 2 double chops, one angled atop of the other. Decorate with extra fresh rosemary sprigs.

Osso Buco My Way

Move over Julia! I am proud of this recipe – the result is delicious, the preparation, easy!

The perfect main course when time is limited – there is no last minute cooking.

4-6 veal shanks

Salt and pepper to taste

Quick-dissolving flour, such as Wondra

1½ cups Marsala

1 (11-ounce) can bouillon soup

2 heads garlic, unpeeled, cloves separated, or 40 peeled cloves

6 whole carrots

Preheat oven to 350 degrees.

The morning of serving, season shanks with salt and pepper and dust with flour. Arrange shanks in a single layer in a casserole dish with a cover.

Add Marsala, bouillon, garlic and carrots. Place a sheet of foil over casserole and then cover with casserole cover.

Bake 1½ hours. Turn off oven and leave shanks in oven all day.

Rewarm in 400 degree oven for 20 minutes. If sauce seems too thin, remove meat and thicken with flour.

Serve shanks topped with carrots and sauce.

The perfect side dish is Baked Polenta with Garlic (page 197).

Veal Fillet with Marsala Mushroom Sauce

I agonized about using this new cut of veal but with Libbie's suggestions, the result was superb!

10-12 veal fillets (Purchased at City Market in North Beach. The butcher removed the white membrane on each side.)

Sea salt and freshly ground pepper to taste

2 sticks butter

6 cloves garlic, mashed

Seasoned Italian bread crumbs

Olive oil

½ cup sweet vermouth

½ cup dry vermouth

½ cup Marsala

MARSALA MUSHROOM SAUCE

8 ounces crimini mushrooms, sliced

8 ounces shiitake mushrooms, sliced

2 tablespoons butter

1 (11-ounce) can bouillon soup

1 soup can brandy

1 soup can Marsala

¾ cup heavy cream

Early in day, flatten fillets a little bit. Season with salt and pepper and form a snail-like roll with each fillet.

Melt butter with garlic and dip veal rolls in mixture. Coat with bread crumbs and sauté in olive oil, keeping rolls intact, until well browned. Deglaze pan with wines and place in oven. Allow to sit in oven all day.

Prepare sauce early in the day. To make sauce, sauté mushrooms in butter until brown; set aside.

Cook bouillon, brandy and Marsala until reduced to 1 cup. Add cream and cook gently until thickened. Stir in mushrooms. Reheat when ready to serve.

When ready to serve, set oven to 350 degrees. Bake 30 to 45 minutes or until done. Serve with sauce spooned over veal.

Veal Rib Chops Piccata

A company dish – serve with risotto and a fine Chardonnay.

6¾ pounds veal rib chops, bones Frenched

1½ cups flour

3 cups seasoned bread crumbs

3 eggs, beaten

Salt and pepper to taste

Olive oil

4 tablespoons butter

2 shallots, finely chopped

⅓ cup chicken broth

⅓ cup white wine or white vermouth

Juice of 2 lemons

1 lemon, thinly sliced

Capers

Preheat oven to 200 degrees.

Flatten each chop between plastic wrap. Place flour, bread crumbs and egg in separate dishes. Season chops with salt and pepper. Dredge chops first in flour, then egg, and finally bread crumbs.

Heat olive oil in a large skillet. Fry chops in oil until golden on one side. Turn and continue frying 5 minutes or until chops are cooked. Place in oven to keep warm.

Wipe skillet clean and return to stove. Add butter and shallots and cook until soft. Add broth, wine, lemon juice and lemon slices. Season with salt and pepper and cook, stirring often, for 5 minutes or until sauce thickens and lemon slices are soft. Add capers and cook until warmed.

Divide chops between 6 warm plates. Spoon sauce, lemon slices and capers over chops.

Veal Roast

I cannot count the times I have served this roast to a captive audience! Making it early in the day allows the flavors to blend and the cook to unwind after a long, hard day at the office!

1 (4-pound) rolled veal roast
Salt and pepper to taste
2 tablespoons olive oil
1 yellow onion
6 cloves garlic
3 carrots
2 cups Marsala wine
1 (11-ounce) can bouillon soup
2 tablespoons Grand Marnier
1 tablespoon cornstarch, dissolved in a small amount of water

Preheat oven to 350 degrees.

Season veal roast with salt and pepper. Brown veal in olive oil in a skillet and transfer to a casserole dish; set aside, reserving skillet.

In a food processor, make a mirepoix of onion, garlic and carrots. Sauté chopped vegetables in reserved skillet, adding extra olive oil, if needed.

Add vegetables to veal. Deglaze skillet with Marsala, bouillon and Grand Marnier and pour over roast.

Cover dish and bake 1 hour. Turn off oven and allow roast to sit in oven all day.

Reheat 1 hour before serving. Remove roast and strain the sauce. (I save the veggies and freeze – then add to spaghetti sauce at a later date.) Add cornstarch to the sauce. Pour over roast, return to oven and cook additional 10 minutes.

This is always a great success!

Veal Stew

Amy perfected this recipe when she was very young. Try it over homemade noodles.

4 carrots, coarsely chopped

1 bunch green onions, coarsely chopped

3 cloves garlic, chopped

3 tablespoons butter

3 tablespoons olive oil

5 pounds veal stew meat

Salt and pepper to taste

1½ cups white wine

¾ cup chicken broth

Preheat oven to 350 degrees.

Sauté carrot, green onions and garlic in butter and oil in a skillet. Transfer to a deep casserole dish; reserve skillet with pan drippings.

Season veal with salt and pepper and sauté in reserved skillet until golden. Place veal atop vegetables. Deglaze the pan with wine and broth and pour over veal.

Cover dish and bake 1½ hours. Remove to a serving dish and keep warm.

Pour cooking sauce into a saucepan and cook until reduced to 1 cup. Pour sauce over meat and serve.

Dish can be made early in the day and reheated before serving.

Zesty Veal Chops

When Pam told me about this recipe, I knew it would be good, given the list of ingredients. Any leftover sauce can be frozen and used over baby back spareribs.

This is an A+ recipe!

Juice and zest of 2 oranges

6 cloves garlic, crushed

3 tablespoons mashed fresh ginger

½ cup molasses

1 cup tamari

6 tablespoons light soy sauce

1 cup rice vinegar

6 tablespoons olive oil

1 teaspoon white pepper

4 (1½- to 2-inch thick) veal chops (buy the best you can find)

Combine all ingredients except veal and mix well. Add veal and marinate at least 4 hours, turning occasionally.

Scrape marinade from chops, transferring marinade to a saucepan. Cook marinade until slightly thickened.

Broil chops until golden on each side; do not overcook.

Nap broiled chops with sauce.

VEGETABLES

Baked Mixed Vegetables

Wendy is more Italian than the Italians. I was privileged to attend one of her cooking classes – this is simply excellent.

3 bell peppers, mixture of red and yellow

4 red potatoes, peeled or unpeeled and cut into wedges

3 ripe tomatoes, cut into wedges

4 red onions, cut into wedges

3 tablespoons olive oil

Salt and pepper to taste

Preheat oven to 400 degrees.

Scrape bell peppers with a vegetable peeler, removing as much skin as possible; do not skip this peeling. Cut peppers into long wedges, discarding seeds and white membrane.

Place pepper wedges, along with potatoes, tomatoes and onions in a large baking dish, making sure not to crowd the vegetables. Drizzle with olive oil and season with salt and pepper.

Bake 25 to 30 minutes, turning every so often. If there is too much liquid in pan after baking, turn oven to 450 degrees and bake 5 to 10 minutes longer.

Asian Vegetable Medley

Colorful – healthful – beautiful.

1 red bell pepper, julienned

2 tablespoons minced fresh ginger

2 cloves garlic, minced

8 ounces shiitake mushrooms, sliced

8 ounces button mushrooms, sliced

4 ounces oyster mushrooms

6 green onions, thinly sliced

2 teaspoons sesame oil

20 ounces fresh spinach

2 tablespoons soy sauce

Lemon wedges

Sauté bell pepper, ginger, garlic, all mushrooms and green onions in sesame oil for 20 minutes. Add spinach and cook 3 minutes longer. Mix in soy sauce.

Transfer to a bowl and serve, passing lemon wedges on the side to squeeze on top.

Asparagus with Parmesan and Bread Crumbs

24 thick asparagus spears, ends cut and peeled

Salt and pepper to taste

4 tablespoons butter, melted, divided

⅓ cup Parmesan cheese

½ cup dry bread crumbs

1 teaspoon lemon zest

Preheat broiler.

Blanch asparagus, drain and dry. Layer blanched asparagus in a gratin dish. Sprinkle with salt and pepper. Drizzle 3 tablespoons melted butter.

Combine Parmesan, bread crumbs and lemon zest. Sprinkle mixture over asparagus, but do not cover the tips. Moisten with remaining 1 tablespoon butter.

Broil until crumb mixture is golden.

Baked Tomatoes with Parmesan Topping

SERVES 8

These are two great recipes that can be baked in separate pans in the same oven at the same time at the same temperature – compatibility!

2 tablespoons olive oil
8 small Roma tomatoes, halved
1 teaspoon sea salt
½ teaspoon ground black pepper
¼ cup chopped flat leaf parsley
¼ cup Parmigiano-Reggiano cheese

Preheat oven to 400 degrees.

Pour oil into a broiler-proof ceramic baking dish. Add tomatoes, turning to coat in oil. Sprinkle with salt and pepper. Top with parsley and cheese. (Can be made 1 day ahead up to this point; cover and chill.)

Bake tomatoes 10 minutes or just until done. Transfer to broiler and cook until cheese begins to color.

The original recipe calls for two 12-ounce baskets of cherry tomatoes.

Baked Asparagus

SERVES 3-4

12 asparagus spears
Olive oil
Grated Parmigianno-Reggiano cheese
Lemon zest

Preheat oven to 400 degrees.

Trim and peel ends of asparagus. Roll sparingly in olive oil. Top with cheese and lemon zest and place in a single layer in a pan.

Bake 10 minutes or until done all the way through (not al dente!)

Barbecue Beans

SERVES 6

I like these beans – the recipe is easy and quick and they are downright delicious!

3 slices bacon, cooked and coarsely chopped

1 onion, chopped

2 cloves garlic, chopped

1 (8-ounce) can tomato sauce

1 cup water

2 tablespoons brown sugar

2 tablespoons molasses

2 tablespoons vinegar

¾ teaspoon dry mustard

1 (15-ounce) can cannelloni beans, rinsed and drained

1 (15-ounce) can red kidney beans, rinsed and drained

1 (15-ounce) can pinto beans, rinsed and drained

Cook bacon in a skillet. Remove bacon and drain, reserving 2 tablespoons bacon drippings in skillet. Sauté onion in hot bacon drippings for 5 minutes. Add garlic, tomato sauce, water, brown sugar, molasses, vinegar and mustard and bring to a boil. Reduce heat and simmer 5 minutes. Stir in all beans and cooked bacon.

Return to a boil. Reduce heat, cover and simmer 5 minutes. Correct seasoning if necessary.

The beans can be served at this point, however, I sometimes pour into a large gratin dish, sprinkle with a tablespoon of brown sugar, cover with foil and bake at 350 degrees for 45 minutes. Then remove foil and bake an additional 15 minutes.

I like to serve these with baby back ribs, roasted yams, crunchy Red Cabbage Salad (page 65) and cornbread.

To make roasted yams, peel and slice in thick French fry strips or half-inch circles. Roll in a generous amount of olive oil, sprinkle with salt and pepper and place on large baking sheet. Bake at 350 degrees for 45 to 50 minutes.

Brussels Sprouts with Ginger and Garlic

This is one of my standbys – everyone loves it and is surprised how much they enjoy Brussels sprouts this way.

1 pound Brussels sprouts

2 tablespoons finely minced fresh ginger

4 cloves garlic, finely minced

3 tablespoons olive oil

Salt and pepper to taste

Using the slicing blade of a food processor, thinly slice Brussels sprouts.

Sauté sprouts, ginger and garlic, stirring occasionally, in olive oil until tender-crisp. Season with salt and pepper.

Great with any meat dish.

Brussels Sprouts with Parmesan

The main dish is forgotten when Libbie prepares this dish.

1 pound Brussels sprouts, boiled gently until just done

2 tablespoons olive oil

½ cup grated Parmesan cheese

Salt and pepper to taste

1 teaspoon garlic powder

Cook Brussels sprouts in gently boiling water until tender; drain.

Sauté cooked sprouts in olive oil for several minutes or until slightly golden. Sprinkle with cheese and season with salt and pepper and garlic powder. Cook 5 minutes and serve.

Creamed Onions

Libbie's onions are as important to our Thanksgiving feast as the turkey!

24 small white onions, unpeeled
4 tablespoons butter
¼ cup flour
½ teaspoon salt
Black pepper to taste
1 (14-ounce) can chicken broth
1 cup light half-and-half
3 tablespoons Parmesan cheese
¼ cup chopped fresh parsley

Place onions in a large saucepan and cover with water. Boil gently for 30 minutes or until fork-tender; drain. When cool enough to touch, slide off onion peels.

Melt butter in a saucepan. Blend in flour, salt and pepper, stirring constantly.

Gradually stir in chicken broth and half-and-half and cook, stirring constantly, until thickened and smooth.

Stir in Parmesan and parsley and blend well. Remove from heat. Add onions and pour mixture into a 1½-quart casserole dish. Cool. Store, covered, in refrigerator until ready to use.

Preheat oven to 350 degrees.

Bake, covered, for 10 to 15 minutes or until heated through and sauce bubbles.

Mashed Carrots and Rutabagas

Couldn't be simpler, couldn't be better.

6 carrots, cut into chunks
3 rutabagas, cut into smaller chunks
Salt and pepper
3 tablespoons butter

Cook carrot and rutabaga until tender. Season with salt and pepper and mash until smooth.

Mix in butter. Serve with anything!

Creamed Spinach

SERVES 4

This is my standby creamed spinach recipe.

6 tablespoons butter

1 (16-ounce) package frozen chopped spinach, thawed, cooked and squeezed dry

1 cup heavy cream

1 cup grated mozzarella cheese

1 teaspoon quick-dissolving flour

Salt and pepper to taste

½ teaspoon garlic powder

Grated nutmeg

Melt butter in a skillet over high heat. Add spinach and half the cream. Cook, stirring in remaining cream a little at a time.

Add cheese and flour and season with salt and pepper, garlic powder and nutmeg.

Serve immediately or heat in a covered casserole when ready to serve.

Malfatti with Marinara Sauce

This is my mother's recipe. An Italian friend told me the word "malfatti" means "badly made". These are not badly made! They are easily made and more easily eaten! A great first course or a light luncheon dish.

1 (10-ounce) package frozen spinach, cooked and squeezed dry

1½ cups ricotta cheese

½ cup Parmigiano-Reggiano cheese, plus extra for topping

1 cup bread crumbs

2 eggs

¼ teaspoon nutmeg

Salt and pepper to taste

Flour

Marinara sauce

Italian parsley sprig for garnish

Combine spinach, both cheeses, bread crumbs, eggs, nutmeg and salt and pepper. Form mixture into balls and flour lightly.

Cook balls in gently boiling water until balls rise to the surface.

Serve topped with marinara sauce and Parmesan cheese. Garnish with parsley.

Eggplant Parmesan

SERVES 6-8

This is Amy's absolutely simple, absolutely delicious rendition of this classic dish. It is on every menu in an Italian restaurant and I am often seduced by its promise, but more times than not, I am disappointed. Not so with this! Very easy preparation.

3 large or 4 small eggplants

Salt

Olive oil

3 red onions, sliced

1 (15-ounce) container refrigerated marinara sauce

1 package shredded Four Italian cheese mixture

Fresh basil or parsley for garnish

Peel eggplant and cut into slices. Spread slices on towels and sprinkle with salt. Cover and weight down for about 30 minutes to remove excess moisture.

Preheat oven to 350 degrees.

Brush slices with olive oil and place on large baking sheets. Bake until tender.

Meanwhile, sauté onions in olive oil without browning for 30 minutes or until very soft.

In large baking dish, layer cooked eggplant, sauce, cheese and onions, reserving ½ cup of the cheese. Sprinkle reserved cheese on top.

Bake at 350 degrees for 40 minutes. Remove from oven and allow to rest 10 minutes. Decorate with chopped fresh basil or parsley.

Onion Gratin

SERVES 6-8

The variety of onions in this gratin makes for an unforgettable dish. A great bring-along for Thanksgiving dinner.

1 stick butter

4 leeks, white and pale green parts only, thoroughly washed and sliced

2 large onions, cut into wedges

8 shallots, halved

2 cloves garlic, minced

2 (10-ounce) packages frozen baby onions, thawed and drained

2 cups heavy cream

3 tablespoons dry bread crumbs

3 tablespoons chopped parsley

Melt butter in a skillet. Add leeks, onion wedges, shallot and garlic and sauté 20 minutes. Add baby onions and cook 10 minutes. Stir in cream and cook 10 minutes longer.

Transfer mixture to a shallow baking dish. At this point, dish can be refrigerated until ready to proceed – bring back to room temperature before baking.

Preheat oven to 425 degrees.

Sprinkle with bread crumbs. Bake 20 minutes or until bread crumbs are golden brown and onions are bubbly. Sprinkle with parsley before serving.

Peppers and Onions

A colorful and delicious vegetable – especially good alongside Steak for All Seasons (page 117)!

¼ cup olive oil

2 large onions, sliced

2 red bell peppers, sliced

1 teaspoons dried marjoram, crumbled

Pinch of dried pepper flakes

Salt and pepper to taste

Heat oil in a skillet. Add onion and sauté 4 minutes. Add bell pepper and sauté about 8 minutes. Stir in marjoram, pepper flakes and salt and pepper.

Red Cabbage and Carrots

Pretty to behold and pretty good for you!

4 medium carrots, julienned

1 small red cabbage, finely shredded

4 tablespoons butter

1 tablespoon minced fresh ginger

1 teaspoon soy sauce

1 teaspoon sugar

Cook carrot 2 minutes in boiling, salted water. Drain and transfer to a bowl. Boil cabbage 2 minutes, drain and transfer to same bowl.

In a small skillet, melt butter. Add carrot, cabbage, ginger, soy and sugar. Sauté 2 minutes. Serve in the company of fried chicken and mashed potatoes.

Roasted Autumn Vegetables

Colorful side dish with in-depth flavor.

1½ pounds small red potatoes, quartered

1 pound shallots, peeled and trimmed, left whole

¼ cup olive oil, plus extra for drizzling

1 bay leaf

½ teaspoon dried thyme

4 cloves garlic, crushed

4 cups butternut squash, cut into ¾-inch cubes

1 tablespoon olive oil

Fresh thyme for garnish

Preheat oven to 375 degrees.

Toss together potatoes, shallots, ¼ cup olive oil, bay leaf, thyme and garlic in a bowl. Spread mixture in a large roasting pan. Roast 25 minutes, shaking pan every 10 minutes.

Drizzle extra olive oil over squash and add to pan. Roast 20 minutes or until tender.

Discard bay leaf. Garnish with fresh thyme.

Roasted Butternut Squash

As the saying goes, I have never met a butternut squash that I did not love – this simple recipe works equally well with yams.

3 pounds butternut squash, about 2 small squash

3 tablespoons olive oil

2 cloves garlic, chopped

Salt and pepper to taste

2 tablespoons unsalted butter, cut into cubes

10 fresh sage leaves

Preheat oven to 475 degrees.

Peel the squash and scoop out the seeds. Cut the flesh into strips about as wide as a finger. Spread squash strips on a baking sheet. Toss with olive oil, garlic and salt and pepper.

Roast 30 minutes, turning once halfway through baking.

Melt butter and cook until it just begins to brown. Add sage leaves and pour over squash. Toss and serve.

Spinach with Pine Nuts and Raisins

So Italian! So delicious!

2 tablespoons raisins

3 tablespoons olive oil

½ small onion, chopped

2 cloves garlic, sliced

2 pounds fresh spinach

Salt and pepper

3 tablespoons pine nuts, toasted

1 tablespoon lemon juice

Thin strips of lemon zest

Soak raisins in warm water for 10 minutes; drain.

Heat olive oil in a pan. Add onion and sauté until soft. Add garlic and cook 1 minute.

Add spinach and cook down for several minutes. Season with salt and pepper. Add raisins, pine nuts, lemon juice and lemon zest.

Spinach Casserole

SERVES 8-10

I love noodles and spinach and garlic and Parmesan and Cheddar and wine and salt and pepper! This is the casserole of all casseroles for a buffet side dish or even a weekday meal.

12 ounces egg noodles, cooked al dente

5 (10-ounce) packages frozen leaf spinach, thawed and squeezed dry

1½ sticks unsalted butter

½ cup flour

2 cloves garlic, minced

3 cups milk, scalded

¼ cup white wine

1½ cups freshly grated Parmesan cheese

3 cups grated sharp Cheddar cheese

½ teaspoon black pepper

Salt to taste

½ cup coarsely chopped walnuts or pecans

½ cup dry Italian-seasoned bread crumbs

Preheat oven to 425 degrees.

Blend noodles and spinach; set aside.

Melt butter in a saucepan. Add flour and cook over medium heat for 1 minute, stirring constantly. Add garlic and cook 3 minutes. Slowly add milk in a stream, whisking until smooth. Add wine and simmer sauce 10 minutes.

Stir noodle mixture into sauce along with cheeses, pepper, salt and nuts. Spoon mixture into a well-greased 9x13-inch baking dish. Sprinkle with bread crumbs.

Bake 20 minutes or until bubbly and crumbs are browned.

Spinach Soufflé

SERVES 8-10

Have you ever wondered why spinach gets such a "bad rap". I know why! It was always served steamed, had a little bit of grit (sand!), and had a bitterness that stuck in the back of your throat. Ugh! The ugly duckling has turned into a swan with this glorious soufflé!

1 small red onion, finely chopped

4 tablespoons butter, divided

4 (10-ounce) packages frozen chopped spinach, cooked and squeezed dry with a cloth

¼ cup flour

2 cups heavy cream

1 cup chicken broth

6 eggs, separated, yolks beaten

¼ teaspoon nutmeg

1 cup Parmesan cheese, divided, plus extra for dusting pan

Salt and pepper to taste

Preheat oven to 325 degrees.

Sauté onion in 2 tablespoons butter until tender. Add spinach, remaining 2 tablespoons butter, flour, cream, broth, beaten egg yolks, nutmeg, ¾ cup Parmesan and salt and pepper. Mix until all is combined completely. Cool.

In batches, process spinach mixture in an electric blender for 15 seconds, scraping sides.

Grease 10-inch soufflé dish and sprinkle with cheese.

Beat egg whites and fold into spinach mixture. Spoon batter into prepared soufflé dish. Sprinkle with remaining ¼ cup cheese.

Set dish in a shallow pan of hot water in the center of the oven. Bake 25 to 30 minutes.

Stuffed Zucchini

It would be easy to make a meal out of this recipe – doubling the recipe is a good idea! Great leftover.

6 medium zucchini

2 tablespoons olive oil, plus extra for brushing on zucchini

1 bunch green onions, sliced

2 tablespoons chopped red bell pepper

1 egg, beaten

2 tablespoons heavy cream

2 tablespoons Parmesan cheese

⅓ cup seasoned bread crumbs, plus extra for topping

1 cup fresh or frozen corn

1 teaspoon dried basil

Salt and pepper to taste

Preheat oven to 400 degrees

Slice zucchini lengthwise in half. Brush with olive oil. Using a small spoon or melon baller, hollow out each half, set outer shells aside.

Chop zucchini centers and sauté in 1 tablespoon oil. Add green onion and bell pepper and continue cooking 1 minute.

Combine egg, cream, cheese, ⅓ cup bread crumbs, corn, basil and salt and pepper in a large bowl. Gently mix in zucchini mixture.

Fill zucchini shells with mixture and place in a well-greased baking dish. Drizzle with remaining 1 tablespoon oil and sprinkle with extra bread crumbs.

Cover with foil. Bake 20 minutes. Uncover and bake 10 to 15 minutes longer or until done.

Whidbey Island John's Broccoli

Oh my! Who would have ever thought broccoli could be this delicious – this dish stands on its own. Make extra to reheat for next day's lunch.

3 tablespoons olive oil
2 pounds broccoli florets
12 whole shallots, halved
4 cloves garlic, slivered
Salt and pepper to taste
3 tablespoons Parmesan cheese

Heat olive oil in a large skillet. Add broccoli and sauté, stirring frequently, for about 2 minutes.

Add shallots, garlic and salt and pepper. Cook about 20 minutes over very low heat. Turn over and cook 15 to 20 minutes longer or until soft throughout. The key is long, very slow cooking.

Transfer to a serving bowl and top with Parmesan.

Keepers
Notes

Accordion Potatoes

SERVES 6

The standard accompaniment to our Steak au Poivre (page 116) – this is one potato that "makes a statement"!

6 baking potatoes, about 4 inches
　long by 2 inches wide

4 tablespoons butter, melted

1¼ teaspoons salt

⅛ teaspoon black pepper

2 cloves garlic, minced

2 tablespoons Parmesan cheese

1 tablespoon chopped fresh
　rosemary

Preheat oven to 425 degrees

Peel potatoes and drop into cold water to prevent darkening. For each potato, insert a skewer lengthwise into a potato ¾-inch from the bottom. Beginning ½-inch from one end of the potato, slice down to skewer at intervals of ¼-inch. Carefully remove potato from skewer and drop back into cold water.

When ready to bake, drain and gently pat dry with paper towels. Arrange potatoes, sliced-side up, in a generously greased 9x13-inch baking dish.

Combine butter, salt, pepper and garlic. Brush potatoes with half of the butter mixture.

Bake 35 to 45 minutes. Pour remaining butter mixture over potatoes. Dust with Parmesan and rosemary and continue to roast, basting occasionally, for 25 minutes or until golden brown and done. Potatoes should have opened like the folds of an accordion into a fan shape.

Basil Potatoes

The method used in preparing these potatoes is what makes them different.

4 pounds potatoes, peeled and cut into ½-inch cubes

¾ cup olive oil

¾ teaspoon dried basil

¾ teaspoon salt

Black pepper to taste

Preheat oven to 350 degrees.

Toss potatoes with olive oil, basil, salt and pepper. Spread potatoes on a greased jelly-roll pan.

Bake 45 minutes without turning. Now turn and continue baking 45 minutes longer or until done.

Perfect Roast Potatoes

There is a reason these potatoes are called "Perfect!" Agree?

2 pounds red potatoes

3 tablespoons extra virgin olive oil

Salt and pepper to taste

2 tablespoons chopped fresh rosemary

2 cloves garlic, minced to a paste

¼ teaspoon salt

Preheat oven to 425 degrees.

Scrub and dry potatoes. Halve potatoes, then cut into ¾-inch wedges. Toss wedges with olive oil and salt and pepper to taste. Arrange wedges, flat-side down, in a baking pan. Cover with foil.

Bake in center of oven for 20 minutes. Remove foil, but do not turn potatoes. Bake 15 minutes longer.

Carefully turn potatoes using a metal spatula. Roast 5 to 10 minutes more. During the last 3 minutes of baking, sprinkle with rosemary.

Meanwhile, blend garlic and ¼ teaspoon salt to a paste in a large bowl. Immediately after removing from oven, add potatoes to bowl and toss to mix. Serve.

Potatoes Dauphinoise

I cannot remember where I found this recipe – someplace French? The preparation is unusual resulting in an outstanding scalloped potato-type dish. Note the absence of cheese which is not missed.

6 medium-size red or Yukon potatoes, peeled and thinly sliced

2 tablespoons salt

2 cloves garlic, mashed

6 tablespoons unsalted butter

2 cups heavy cream

½ cup milk

Pinch of black pepper

Pinch of nutmeg

Preheat oven to 350 degrees.

Toss potatoes with salt in a bowl. Let stand 20 minutes. There will be a substantial amount of brown liquid which is exuded from the potatoes. Drain and rinse thoroughly. Pat dry.

Combine garlic, butter, cream, milk, pepper and nutmeg in a saucepan. Bring to almost a boil, watching carefully. (It has boiled over on me several times!)

Arrange potato slices in a baking dish. Pour cream mixture over all. Place dish on a baking sheet.

Bake 1 hour or until potatoes are tender. Allow to stand for 10 minutes before serving.

Very, very good.

Potatoes with Leeks

Unusual and unusually good!

5 tablespoons unsalted butter, divided

2 large leeks, white and tender green parts, thoroughly rinsed and thinly sliced

2 tablespoons chopped fresh parsley

6 medium-size red potatoes, peeled and thinly sliced

Salt and pepper to taste

1 cup chicken broth

Preheat oven to 450 degrees.

Melt 2 tablespoons butter in a large ovenproof skillet. Add leeks and sauté 5 minutes or until soft. Stir in parsley and cook 1 minute. Transfer leeks to a separate dish and set aside, return skillet to heat.

Melt 2 tablespoons butter in skillet. Remove from heat. Layer half of potato slices and half of leek mixture in skillet. Repeat layers. Season each layer with salt and pepper. Add broth to skillet. Dot top with remaining 1 tablespoon butter.

Bake 30 minutes or until potatoes are done.

Puffed Potatoes with Parmesan

SERVES 4

Have you ever met a potato you did not like! Libbie introduced us to this sensational recipe. They will make a weekday meal memorable.

2 large baking potatoes, scrubbed
2 cloves garlic, chopped
3 tablespoons olive oil
½ cup Parmesan cheese
Salt and pepper to taste
2 tablespoons minced fresh parsley

And now the fun begins!

Preheat oven to 400 degrees

Cut each potato lengthwise into 4 slices. Rub the cut sides together until a starchy white liquid appears on the surface. (This starch on the potato is what causes them to puff.) Place slices, cut-side up, on a greased jelly-roll pan.

Bake in the center of the oven until potatoes are puffed.

While the potatoes are baking, cook the garlic in olive oil for several minutes. Strain through a fine sieve, reserving the oil.

Sprinkle Parmesan on the potatoes. Bake 2 minutes longer or until cheese is melted.

Remove potatoes from pan and place on serving dish. Sprinkle with salt and pepper and parsley and drizzle reserved oil over all.

Red Potatoes with Mint and Garlic

A great potato salad alternative.

8 cloves garlic, finely mined

1 cup olive oil

1 bunch fresh mint, minced

5 pounds red potatoes, small and equal-sized

2 tablespoons coarse kosher salt

Black pepper to taste

Mint sprigs for garnish

The night before serving, combine garlic, olive oil and mint in a dish; set aside.

The day of serving, preheat oven to 350 degrees.

Wash potatoes and prick all over with a fork. Place potatoes on an ungreased pan. Bake 1 hour. Remove from oven and cool; do not refrigerate. Cut potatoes in half.

To serve, remove most of the mint from the oil. Toss oil with potato halves. Sprinkle with salt and pepper. Serve on a platter garnished with mint sprigs.

Roquefort Potato Gratin

SERVES 12

A definite crowd pleaser.

6 pounds russet potatoes, peeled and sliced

Salt and pepper to taste

2 cups heavy cream

5 ounces Roquefort cheese, crumbled

½ cup dry bread crumbs

1½ teaspoons chopped fresh rosemary

4 tablespoons butter, cut into small pieces

Preheat oven to 425 degrees.

Layer potato slices in a greased 15x10x2-inch glass baking dish, sprinkling each layer with salt and pepper.

Bring cream to a boil, watching carefully. Reduce to medium heat and whisk in cheese until cheese melts. Pour cream mixture over potatoes. Cover with foil. Bake 1 hour or until potatoes are tender.

Preheat broiler.

Mix bread crumbs with rosemary and sprinkle over potatoes. Dot with butter. Broil potatoes 4 minutes or until butter melts and crumbs are golden, watching closely. Let stand 10 minutes before serving.

Scalloped Potatoes with Spinach

A great dish – a lovely accompaniment to grilled steak or chicken.

4 tablespoons butter

1 large onion, chopped

2 (10-ounce) packages frozen spinach, thawed and drained

Salt and pepper to taste

1½ cups heavy cream

¾ cup chicken broth

¾ cup white wine

6 large russet potatoes, thinly sliced

½ teaspoon ground nutmeg

1 cup grated white Cheddar cheese

Preheat oven to 400 degrees.

Melt butter in a skillet. Add onion and sauté until soft. Add spinach and cook until liquid has evaporated. Season with salt and pepper; set aside.

Mix cream, broth and wine in a bowl.

Arrange one-third of potato slices in the bottom of a 9x13-inch glass baking dish. Season with salt and pepper and a sprinkling of the nutmeg. Top with half of the spinach mixture. Pour one-third of cream mixture over the top. Repeat layering with one-third of potatoes, salt and pepper, nutmeg, remaining spinach mixture and the remaining potatoes. Pour remaining cream mixture over all.

Bake 45 minutes. Top with cheese and bake 15 minutes longer or until potatoes are tender and cheese is golden. Let stand 15 minutes before serving.

Sweet Potato Gratin with Ginger

1 tablespoon crystallized ginger
½ medium onion
1 clove garlic
3 medium yams, thinly sliced
3 medium Yukon potatoes, thinly sliced
Salt and pepper to taste
1 cup heavy cream
1 cup chicken broth
1 stick butter
¼ teaspoon nutmeg

Preheat oven to 375 degrees.

Chop ginger in a food processor. Add onion and garlic and process until finely chopped.

Layer yam and potato slices with ginger mixture, repeating layers twice to form 3 layers. Season each layer with salt and pepper.

Heat cream, broth and butter and pour over layers. Sprinkle with nutmeg. Cover dish with foil.

Bake 15 minutes. Remove foil and bake 15 minutes longer.

Outstanding!

Sweet Potato Pancakes

MAKES 12 PANCAKES

Pork chops, sautéed spinach and sweet potato pancakes will make everyone very happy!

1 large yam
1 small yellow onion
2 large eggs
2 tablespoons flour
⅛ teaspoon cardamom
Salt and pepper to taste
3 tablespoons vegetable oil

Shred yam and onion. Wrap in a towel and squeeze out moisture.

Mix eggs, flour, cardamom and salt and pepper a bowl. Stir in yam and onion and mix well.

Heat oil in a pan. Drop potato batter by tablespoon into pan. Cook about 1 minute on each side.

Keepers
NOTES

Bowtie Pasta with Tuna

Do you remember Mom and Dad off for the evening and the children left with macaroni and cheese with tuna? We loved it then, but the this rendition is for "grown up" tastes and Mom and Dad would rather stay home for this treat!

2 (6-ounce) cans oil-packed tuna, drained, oil reserved

½ cup dry bread crumbs

½ cup Parmigiano-Reggiano cheese

1 pound bowtie pasta (farfalle), cooked al dente and drained

3 (10-ounce) containers store-bought refrigerated Alfredo sauce

2 cups thinly sliced green onions

1 cup frozen petite peas

2 teaspoons dried oregano

2 teaspoons lemon zest

Preheat oven to 400 degrees.

Mix ¼ cup reserved tuna oil with bread crumbs and cheese; set aside.

Combine cooked pasta with Alfredo sauce, green onions, peas, oregano and lemon zest in a bowl. Transfer to a 3-quart oval baking dish. Sprinkle with crumb mixture.

Bake 20 minutes or until piping hot and bread crumbs are golden.

Easy, Easy, Delicious, Delicious.

Baked Capellini

SERVES 8

There are times a pasta dish would round out the menu but you do not want the last minute preparation. This works as a wonderful side dish.

1 pound capellini (angel hair) pasta

3 tablespoons butter, softened

1½ cups freshly grated Parmigiano-Reggiano cheese

1½ cups heavy cream

Salt and pepper to taste

Preheat oven to 400 degrees.

Cook pasta in boiling water until barely al dente; drain and return to pot. Stir in small amounts of butter at a time. Add cheese and cream and season with salt and pepper. Spread in a greased 9x13-inch baking dish.

Bake 20 to 30 minutes or until golden. Cut into squares and serve.

Besto Pesto

Bill is a great cook! He cooks with love and passion! Lime juice cuts the richness – this dish is not for sissies!

1 bunch basil, leaves only

6 cloves garlic, finely minced

4 tablespoons butter

½ cup olive oil

1 (3-ounce) package cream cheese, softened

¼ cup pine nuts, slightly toasted

½ cup hot water

Juice of 1 lime

Salt and pepper to taste

12 ounces linguine, cooked al dente and drained

Parmigiano-Reggiano cheese

Place basil leaves, garlic, butter, olive oil, cream cheese and pine nuts in a food processor and blend until smooth. Blend in water and lime juice. Season with salt and pepper.

Mix pesto into cooked linguine and top with lots of cheese.

Cheese and Macaroni

It does seem that there is more cheese than macaroni in this superb soul food.

2 tablespoons butter

3 tablespoons flour

2¼ cups milk, heated

½ cup grated sharp Cheddar cheese

¼ cup mascarpone cheese

Salt and pepper to taste

Pinch of nutmeg

8 ounces penne pasta, cooked al dente and drained

¼ cup grated Parmesan

Preheat oven to 400 degrees.

Melt butter in a saucepan. Stir in flour and cook several minutes. Slowly add milk and blend until smooth. Add Cheddar and mascarpone cheeses and season with salt and pepper and nutmeg.

Combine cheese sauce with cooked penne. Transfer to a 9-inch square glass dish. Sprinkle with Parmesan. Bake 15 minutes. Place under broiler and cook until top is brown, watching carefully.

Creamy Tomato Sauce

Uncle John's favorite! And ours! And now, yours!

3 whole cloves garlic

1 (28-ounce) can crushed tomatoes

1 whole yellow onion

1 stick butter

1 cup heavy cream

12 ounces penne pasta, cooked al dente

Parmigiano-Reggiano cheese

Combine whole garlic cloves, tomatoes, whole onion and butter in large saucepan and simmer 45 minutes. Remove onion and garlic, reserving for another use if desired.

Meanwhile, pour cream into a separate saucepan. Cook until reduce by half.

Mix cream with tomatoes. Serve over cooked penne with Parmigiano-Reggiano on the side.

Crab and Asparagus Linguini

SERVES 3-4

Italians eat pasta as one course in a several-course meal, eating half the amount we eat as a main course. Not so with this dish – it is a meal unto itself – company fare at its finest!

6 fresh asparagus spears

1 stick butter, divided

2 tablespoons lemon zest

2 tablespoons dry vermouth

1⅔ cups heavy cream

Dashes of cayenne pepper

12 ounces fresh linguini pasta, cooked al dente

½ cup Parmigiano-Reggiano cheese

Salt and pepper to taste

1 pound fresh crabmeat, reserve whole legs for garnish

Parsley sprigs for garnish

Trim and peel asparagus spears and cut into 1-inch pieces. Blanch asparagus 3 to 5 minutes; drain and set aside.

Melt 4 tablespoons butter in a large skillet. Add lemon zest and cook 2 minutes. Add vermouth and cook 2 minutes. Add cream and continue to cook and stir 2 minutes. Add cayenne to taste.

Mix cream sauce with cooked linguini. Cut remaining 4 tablespoons butter into pieces. Add butter pieces, cheese, salt and pepper, crab and blanched asparagus. Mix gently to incorporate all of the ingredients.

Serve in warm dishes garnished with whole crab legs and a sprig of parsley!

Creamy Pasta with Garlic Prawns

SERVES 4

This is another Libbie specialty – there is an absence of all table conversation when one is eating this dish! Oh, perhaps one can hear an occasional "yum" but that is all! Easy to prepare, company special, beautiful to behold.

PASTA

2 bunches green onions, sliced

4 tablespoons butter

1 tablespoon olive oil

3 cloves garlic, chopped

1 pint heavy cream

½ cup Parmigiano-Reggiano cheese

12 ounces capellini or linguine pasta, cooked al dente

PRAWNS

24 large prawns

Flour

Black pepper

¼ cup olive oil

10 cloves garlic, chopped (Libbie uses more!)

1½ tablespoons lemon juice

1 teaspoon lemon zest

2 tablespoons butter

2 tablespoons finely chopped fresh parsley

Sauté green onions in butter and olive oil until softened. Add garlic and cook 20 seconds; do not allow garlic to take on any color.

Add cream and cook until mixture bubbles. Add cheese. Mix sauce into cooked pasta.

To prepare prawns, pat dry prawns and roll in flour seasoned with pepper. Sauté on 1 side in olive oil for 2 minutes. Turn shrimp over and add garlic, lemon juice and zest. Cook 2 to 3 minutes. Add butter and parsley.

To serve, mound pasta in center of plate. Surround with prawns.

A sprig of parsley and perhaps julienne zucchini and yellow and red bell pepper add the right color to the presentation and palate.

Crab and Shrimp Lasagna

SERVES 8

This is not classic "lasagna" – these are lasagna roll-ups that make a lovely presentation, take time but are worth the effort. It is a recipe that you will use over and over when you want to impress!

16 extra wide lasagna noodles

SAUCE
2 tablespoons olive oil
1 onion, chopped
4 cloves garlic, minced
2 (28-ounce) cans Italian-style tomatoes
⅓ cup chopped fresh basil
1 tablespoon chopped fresh thyme
2 teaspoons dried oregano
1 cup heavy cream

FILLING
2 tablespoons olive oil
1 onion, chopped
1 clove garlic, minced
12 ounces raw shrimp, peeled, deveined and chopped
⅓ cup chopped fresh basil
¾ teaspoon dried oregano
½ teaspoon dried red pepper flakes
1½ cups ricotta cheese
¾ cup grated provolone cheese
⅓ cup Parmigiano-Reggiano cheese
8 ounces fresh crabmeat
Salt and pepper to taste
1 egg, beaten

Preheat oven to 350 degrees.

Cook noodles in boiling salted water until al dente. Cool in a bowl of cold water. When ready to assemble, drain and cut noodles into 8-inch lengths.

For sauce, heat oil in a large skillet. Add onion and sauté until softened. Add garlic, tomatoes, basil, thyme and oregano. Bring to a boil. Reduce heat and simmer about 45 minutes; set aside. When cool, purée sauce in a blender and return to same pot. Add cream and simmer 15 minutes.

To prepare filling, heat olive oil in a large skillet. Add onion and cook until softened. Mix in garlic and cook 3 minutes. Add shrimp and sauté just until opaque. Stir in basil, oregano and pepper flakes; cool.

Mix ricotta, provolone and Parmesan cheeses and crabmeat. Combine with shrimp mixture. Season with salt and pepper and mix in egg.

To assemble, spread a scant ⅓ cup filling over each noodle, leaving a ½-inch border on all sides. Starting at a short end, roll up each noodle, jelly-roll style.

CRAB AND SHRIMP LASAGNA — CONTINUED

Spread 1 cup sauce in the bottom of a greased 9x13-inch baking dish. Place lasagna rolls, seam-side down, in dish. Pour remaining sauce over the top. Cover with foil. Lasagna can be prepared to this point up to 1 day ahead and refrigerated until ready to bake.

Bake, covered, for 45 minutes or until heated through.

Fettucine with Mushrooms, Peas and Prosciutto

SERVES 4

Delicious – colorful – great first course!

1 tablespoon olive oil

10 ounces white mushrooms, thinly sliced

1 cup heavy cream

Salt and pepper to taste

6 ounces thickly sliced prosciutto, cut into ¼-inch strips

1 cup frozen petite peas, thawed

1 tablespoon unsalted butter

8 ounces white and green fettuccine pasta, cooked al dente and drained

½ cup Parmigiano-Reggiano cheese

Heat olive oil until hot in a large skillet. Add mushrooms and cook until all moisture evaporates. Stir in cream and season with salt and pepper. Cook, stirring occasionally, until cream is reduced by half.

Add prosciutto and peas. Stir in butter and remove from heat.

Add pasta and half the cheese. Toss over low heat. Adjust seasoning and serve topped with remaining cheese.

Crispy Crab Ravioli

SERVES 4

I must admit this is a rather labor-intensive recipe. There are four steps; making the sauce, then the filling, stuffing the ravioli and, finally, baking. Several steps can be done ahead of time. They are fantastic. I said Fantastic!

SAUCE

1 tablespoon vegetable oil

Crab shells

1 leek, white only, chopped

1 stalk celery, finely chopped

2 shallots, chopped

1 cup white wine

1 teaspoon tomato paste

1 cup packed fresh basil leaves

1 tablespoon fresh thyme, or
    1 teaspoon dried

3 black peppercorns

1 cup fish stock or clam juice

3 tablespoons brandy

½ cup heavy cream

Salt and pepper to taste

In a large skillet, heat oil. Add crab shells and brown about 15 minutes, mashing shells down with a wooden spoon. Stir in leek, celery, shallots, wine, tomato paste, basil, thyme and peppercorns. Simmer 10 minutes until reduced to ½ cup.

Add stock and brandy and simmer 5 minutes. Pour mixture through a sieve, pressing hard on solids.

Add cream and simmer, uncovered, for about 3 minutes. Season with salt and pepper. May be made up to 2 days ahead and stored in refrigerator with surface covered with plastic wrap.

MAKES ABOUT 2 CUPS SAUCE.

FILLING

2 tablespoons butter

1 shallot, chopped

5 shiitake mushrooms, stems
    removed, thinly sliced

2 small zucchini, julienne to
    ¾-inch

1 cup fresh crabmeat

½ cup heavy cream

3 tablespoons chopped fresh
    Italian parsley

Salt and pepper to taste

For filling, cook shallots, mushrooms and zucchini in butter in a large skillet for about 6 minutes. Add crab and cream and simmer 4 minutes. Add parsley, salt and pepper.

Cover and chill at least 2 hours or up to 1 day.

Preheat oven to 450 degrees.

CRISPY CRAB RAVIOLI — CONTINUED

ASSEMBLY
1 egg
Water
24 won ton wrappers

To assemble, in a small bowl, beat together egg and water for an egg wash. Place 1 wrapper on lightly floured surface and place a heaping tablespoon of filling in center. Lightly brush edge of wrapper with egg wash and top with a second wrapper. Press down to seal firmly. Proceed with remaining wrappers, making 12 ravioli total.

Arrange ravioli in a single layer in a baking pan. Brush tops with egg wash. Bake 8 minutes.

Meanwhile, gently warm sauce. Divide warmed sauce among 4 dishes. Top each with 3 ravioli and decorate with sprigs of dill or a spring flower or two.

Lemon Cream Pasta

SERVES 6

Linda is a wonderful cook! We were the guests of honor at an intimate dinner in her charming Mill Valley home and the conversation ceased when we all dug into this superb first course.

1⅓ cups heavy cream

1 tablespoon lemon zest

1 stick unsalted butter, cut into pieces

1½ cups freshly grated Parmesan cheese

Freshly grated nutmeg to taste

Salt and pepper to taste

1 pound capellini pasta, cooked al dente and drained

In a small heavy saucepan, combine cream and lemon zest. Bring to a boil and cook 3 minutes. Reduce heat to low and whisk in butter, piece by piece, until melted.

Add Parmesan, nutmeg and salt and pepper, whisking until the Parmesan is melted.

Serve sauce over drained pasta.

Pasta Verde

This is a great "side dish" pasta – easy, easy, easy! Delicious, delicious, delicious!

6 tablespoons butter

1 bunch green onions, chopped, including green part

4 cloves garlic, minced

1½ cups heavy cream

12 ounces angel hair pasta, cooked al dente and drained

1 cup Parmigiano-Reggiano cheese

Melt butter in large skillet. Add green onions and cook 2 minutes. Add garlic, mixing well. Add cream and bring to a rapid boil, watching all the while. Cook until slightly thickened.

Add cooked pasta and cheese.

Italian Soul Food.

Libbie's Linguini with Red Clam Sauce

SERVES 6

What's for dinner! No time to shop! Go to the cupboard, pull out a few cans, and produce this most outstanding pasta dish – in minutes! Libbie teaches nursing, serves a sit down dinner every evening, entertains often and beautifully, but when time is limited, no one suffers – this pasta could not be better if you had all the time in the world! And the leftovers, if any – ooh-la-la!

1 onion, finely chopped

2 tablespoons olive oil

6 canned anchovy fillets, drained and chopped

6 cloves garlic, finely chopped

½ teaspoon dried red pepper flakes

1 (14½-ounce) can diced tomatoes

1 (14½-ounce) can tomato purée

4 (6½-ounce) cans chopped clams (Neptune brand is excellent)

½ cup dry red wine

1 pound linguine, cooked al dente and drained

Salt and pepper to taste

¼ cup chopped fresh parsley

Parmesan cheese

Gently sauté onion in olive oil until is soft but not golden. Add anchovies, garlic and red pepper flakes and sauté 2 minutes. Mix in tomatoes, tomato purée, clams with juice and wine. Bring sauce to a boil. Reduce heat and simmer about 5 minutes.

Add linguine to sauce and toss. Season with salt and pepper. Transfer to a large platter and sprinkle with parsley. Pass Parmesan on the side.

Italians say no cheese on seafood pasta, however, it is delicious in this recipe.

Meaty Spaghetti Sauce

Everyone has a special spaghetti sauce recipe. I have given myself Three Stars on this one!

1 small onion, finely chopped

1 small leek, white only, finely chopped

½ cup coarsely chopped carrot

2 tablespoons olive oil

1 pound ground sirloin

2 cloves garlic, chopped

½ cup red wine

1 (28-ounce) can crushed tomatoes

1 (28-ounce) can plum tomatoes, puréed in food processor

½ cup dried porcini mushrooms, pulverized in blender

4 tablespoons butter

1 teaspoon sugar

Pinch of baking soda

1 teaspoon dried thyme

1 teaspoon dried marjoram

Salt and pepper to taste

Sauté onion, leek and carrot in olive oil in a skillet until soft; remove from pan and set aside.

In the same pan, sauté ground sirloin, adding extra oil, if needed. When meat has lost its color, add sautéed vegetables and garlic and mix well.

Add wine and all tomatoes and cook gently for 1 hour, stirring occasionally.

Stir in mushrooms, butter, sugar, baking soda, thyme and marjoram and continue to cook 30 minutes. Taste and season as needed with salt and pepper.

Serve over any al dente-cooked pasta anytime to anyone and know this is the Best!

Mushroom and Sausage Fettuccine

SERVES 4

All the right ingredients in this special dish. It stands on its own and needs only a green salad, poached pears, biscotti and a nice wine to throw a great weeknight party!

1 pound mild Italian sausages, casings removed

6 ounces button mushrooms, sliced

6 ounces shiitake mushrooms, stem removed, sliced

1 bunch green onions, sliced

¼ cup chopped fresh Italian parsley

2 tablespoons chopped fresh basil, or 2 teaspoons dried

1 teaspoon chopped fresh or dried rosemary

3 cloves garlic, minced

12 ounces fettuccine pasta, cooked al dente and drained

1½ cups chicken broth

1½ cups Parmigiano-Reggiano cheese, divided

Sauté sausage until cooked through, breaking up clumps with the back of a spoon. (My little secret is throwing the meat into the processor and processing a few seconds to remove the clumps – it works!)

Transfer sausage to a bowl, pouring off all but 2 tablespoons of the pan drippings. Add all mushrooms, green onions, parsley, basil, rosemary and garlic to pan drippings and sauté about 8 minutes.

Return sausage to pan. Add drained fettuccine, broth and 1 cup cheese. Toss 4 minutes or until sauce thickens. Adjust seasonings as needed.

Serve with remaining ½ cup cheese.

Orecchiette with Scallops

SERVES 6

This "primi piatti" is delicate and delicious with scallops, however, I have substituted prawns or clams, or a combination of all – with equally delectable results.

2 shallots, finely diced

2 tablespoons olive oil

2 tablespoons butter

2 cloves garlic, crushed

3 zucchini, finely diced

½ pound sea scallops (if substituting prawns, slice into thirds)

½ cup dry vermouth

1 (8-ounce) bottle clam juice

1 pound orechiette pasta, cooked al dente and drained

3 tomatoes, peeled, seeded and finely diced

¾ teaspoon fresh or dried thyme

1 ounce fresh basil, chiffonade (stack leaves, roll tightly, cut thinly)

Salt and pepper to taste

Chopped Italian parsley

Sauté shallots in olive oil and butter until limp. Add garlic, stir, and immediately remove from pan; set aside.

In same pan, sauté zucchini until soft. Set aside atop shallot mixture.

Pat scallops dry with paper towels. In same pan (you may need to add a little more butter and oil) sauté scallops 2 minutes on each side. Do not mix around to allow better browning. Remove and set aside.

Add vermouth and clam juice to the pan and cook down until reduced by half. Add drained pasta to pan along with sautéed vegetables and scallops. Add tomatoes, thyme and basil. Season with salt and pepper and mix thoroughly.

Serve with a sprinkling of chopped parsley.

Very special!

Pasta Belvedere

SERVES 6

I love being invited to the home of my special friends in Belvedere. Kathy and John can produce the most wonderful dinners that are relaxed and casual yet absolutely elegant! This pasta dish further explains their style!

½ cup extra virgin olive oil

6 Roma tomatoes, coarsely diced

8 ounces fontina cheese, cut into small cubes

8 ounces Monterey Jack cheese, cut into small cubes

½ cup Parmigiano-Reggiano cheese

¼ cup small capers, rinsed

½ cup shredded fresh basil

1 (2-ounce) can anchovy fillets, drained and minced

Dash of dried red pepper flakes

Black pepper to taste

1 tablespoon dried oregano

1 pound linguine pasta

Combine all ingredients except pasta in a large bowl. Let stand at room temperature at least 2 hours.

Cook pasta until al dente; drain. Toss hot pasta with uncooked sauce.

The dicing and chopping takes a little time but is absolutely worth it!

Penne with Oven-Roasted Tomatoes

This is one of my all-time favorite pasta dishes – the tomatoes are delicious. I oftentimes roast pounds and pounds and freeze recipe portions in small baggies. I bless the lady who gave me this recipe, as will you!

¼ cup olive oil

4 ounces pancetta, cut into 1-inch strips

3 zucchini, julienned into 2-inch strips

Salt and pepper to taste

1½ cups Oven-Roasted Tomatoes (see below)

1 tablespoon butter

2 tablespoons fresh thyme

¼ cup chopped fresh Italian parsley

12 ounces penne pasta, or other small tubular pasta, cooked al dente and drained

Pecorino cheese

Heat olive oil in large skillet. Add pancetta and sauté to render the fat. Add zucchini and salt and pepper and sauté 5 minutes. Add tomatoes and cook 1 minute. Stir in butter. Toss with thyme and parsley.

Gently mix in drained pasta. Serve with pecorino cheese on the side.

Pecorino cheese is a little zestier than Parmesan.

OVEN-ROASTED TOMATOES

6 tomatoes, cut in half

3 cloves garlic, thinly sliced

½ tablespoon salt

½ tablespoon black pepper

½ tablespoon sugar

1 tablespoon dried oregano

Olive oil

Preheat oven to 250 degrees.

Arrange tomatoes on a parchment-lined baking pan. Tuck garlic into tomatoes. Sprinkle with salt, pepper, sugar and oregano. Drizzle with olive oil.

Bake 4 hours without turning tomatoes. Remove from oven and cool. Discard tomato peel and garlic.

Prawns and Capellini

SERVES 4-6

This is one of Libbie's specialties. Quick to prepare – we always marvel how a dish this simple to prepare can be so outstanding!

PRAWNS

1 large package (21/25 count) cleaned and deveined prawns

Flour

Black pepper

Olive oil

10 cloves garlic, chopped

Juice of ½ lemon

Zest of 2 lemons

Fresh parsley, very finely chopped

2 tablespoons butter

PASTA

2 bunches green onions, sliced

4 tablespoons butter

2 tablespoons olive oil

2 cloves garlic, chopped

1 pint heavy cream

½ cup Parmigiano-Reggiano cheese

1 pound capellini pasta, cooked al dente and drained

Parsley sprigs and lemon wedges for garnish

Pat dry prawns. Dust prawns with flour seasoned with pepper in a bag, patting off excess.

Sauté prawns in olive oil on one side for 2 minutes or until crisp. Turn prawns and add garlic, lemon juice and zest and cook 2 to 3 minutes longer.

Stir in parsley and butter and set aside.

For the pasta, briefly sauté green onions in butter and olive oil until softened. Stir in garlic but do not allow garlic to brown.

Add cream and mix well. Gently blend in cheese. Toss with drained pasta.

Serve pasta on heated plates, surrounded with prawns and garnished with parsley sprigs and lemon wedges.

Perfect Pasta

There is no pasta like homemade pasta for certain sauces. We love "store-bought" Italian dry pastas, but there are times just getting out the pasta machine and "going for it" satisfies more than the appetite! Dear Warren, who could only barbecue, learned how to roll out the pasta. He was meticulous, he was proud, we raved over his talent, we loved every morsel, we loved every minute!

3 cups unbleached flour, plus extra for rolling out dough

3 eggs

1 teaspoon salt

1 tablespoon olive oil

1 tablespoon water, or more if needed

Blend all ingredients in a food processor until mixture just begins to form a ball. Add more water, drop by drop, if dough seems too dry. The dough should be firm, not sticky. Total blending time should be about 15 seconds.

Remove dough and form into a large patty. Cover with plastic wrap and set aside at room temperature 45 minutes.

Set the smooth rollers of a pasta machine at the highest number; rollers will be wide apart.

Divide dough into small pieces and flatten into rough rectangles; cover.

Working with one rectangle at a time, dust with flour and feed through the rollers. Fold the rectangle in half and feed through rollers 8 times, folding in half each time. Continue turning the dial down one notch and feed the dough through until the lowest notch is reached. Roll each dough rectangle in the same manner.

Cut dough into desired shape; the machine has rollers for linguini and fettuccini. Cut wide strips for pappardelle by hand. This pasta will cook in just over a minute! Divine!

Ravioli with Gorgonzola Filling

An experiment using the bounty of summer's sweet white corn and treasures from the refrigerator produced the following treat.

4 ounces ricotta cheese
3 ounces Gorgonzola cheese
½ beaten egg
1 ear fresh white corn kernels
3 tablespoons chopped walnuts
½ package wonton wrappers

Combine all ingredients except wonton wrappers to make a filling. Using filling and wonton wrappers, proceed as instructed in directions for Ravioli à la Casa (page 188).

Top with a rich and creamy sauce and a generous sprinkling of Parmesan.

It's fun to experiment with ravioli – they truly are user-friendly. I sometimes omit the boiling process and it works! Simply place the ravioli in a single layer in a large roasting pan. Pour a light tomato sauce over the top, cover pan with foil and bake at 400 degrees for 15 minutes.

Another time, place the ravioli in the large baking pan, add chicken broth halfway up, not submerging the ravioli. Sprinkle with Parmesan, cover with foil and bake at 400 degrees for 15 minutes. Serve in wide bowls with the broth and additional cheese.

And, another time, do not cover with foil, sprinkle with Parmesan and bake. The ravioli are crispy and slightly golden on top. Delicious.

Ravioli à la Casa

MAKES ABOUT 5 DOZEN

Many hands make light work! Remember those words? Grandparents, parents, children, neighbors – everyone wants to lend a hand in assembling homemade ravioli.

1 package thin wonton wrapper

Sausage Spinach Filling (see page 189)

2 egg whites, beaten

Creamy Tomato Sauce (see page 189)

Freshly grated Parmigiano-Reggiano cheese

Place 1 wrapper on a lightly floured board. Evenly spread a rounded tablespoon of filling to within about ⅜-inch of edges. Brush edges with egg white. Cover with another wrapper and press edges well to seal. If desired, run a pastry wheel just inside edges to make a decorative edge. Discard trimmings.

Place ravioli in a single layer on a flour-dusted baking sheet and cover with plastic wrap. Cook immediately or chill up to 4 hours.

To cook, bring 4 quarts of water to boil. Add about one-third of the ravioli and boil gently for about 3 minutes. With a large slotted spoon, lift out a ravioli and test for doneness. When done, remove remaining ravioli and pat dry with paper towel if they seem too wet. Repeat process with remaining ravioli. Nap ravioli with Creamy Tomato Sauce and sprinkle generously with cheese.

RAVIOLI À LA CASA — CONTINUED

SAUSAGE SPINACH FILLING

6 ounces mild Italian sausage, casings removed

1 (10-ounce) package frozen chopped spinach, thawed and squeezed dry

2 cups ricotta cheese

2 egg yolks

1 cup Parmigiano-Reggiano cheese

⅛ teaspoon black pepper

¼ teaspoon crushed fennel seed

¼ teaspoon dried oregano

Sauté sausage over low heat until golden and crumbly; drain off any fat.

Mix sausage with remaining ingredients. Use at once or cover and chill as long as overnight.

CREAMY TOMATO SAUCE

1 medium onion, finely chopped

4 cloves garlic, mashed

3 tablespoons olive oil

2 (28-ounce) plus 1 (14-ounce) cans Italian-style tomatoes, coarsely chopped

1½ tablespoons dried basil

1 cup chicken broth

½ cup heavy cream

Salt and pepper to taste

In a large skillet, sauté onion and garlic in olive oil until onion is limp, but not brown.

Add tomatoes, basil and broth and simmer, uncovered, for 20 minutes or until sauce is slightly thickened.

Stir in cream and season with salt and pepper.

Use at once or cover and chill up to 24 hours.

Sausage and Zucchini Macaroni and Cheese

SERVES 4

If you brought this casserole to the church social, they would sanctify you!

1 tablespoon olive oil

4 Italian sausages, casings removed

1 onion, chopped

3 zucchini, cut into 1½-inch strips

Salt and pepper to taste

1 cup heavy cream

1 teaspoon dried oregano

8 ounces fontina cheese, grated, divided

8 ounces penne pasta

Preheat oven to 375 degrees.

Heat oil in a skillet and add sausage. Cook until no longer pink, breaking up with fork. Transfer to bowl.

Add onion to skillet and cook 5 minutes or until soft. Add zucchini and salt and pepper and sauté until almost tender. Return sausage to skillet. Add cream and oregano and bring to boil.

Add half of the cheese and stir until melted.

Meanwhile, cook pasta al dente. Drain well and return to pot. Add cream sauce to drained pasta. Correct seasoning and transfer to a greased 3-quart casserole dish. Top with remaining cheese.

Bake 15 to 20 minutes. This recipe can be doubled, tripled, quadrupled!

Seafood Pasta

Libbie's yummy creation!

½ pound rock shrimp

½ pound bay scallops, pat dry with paper towel

½ pound orange roughy, cut into small pieces

3 tablespoons olive oil

1 bunch green onions, chopped

6 cloves garlic, minced

¼ cup dry vermouth

2 cups chopped tomatoes, drained if using canned

1 cup heavy cream

½ cup Parmigiano-Reggiano cheese, plus extra for topping

Dried red pepper flakes

1 pound angel hair pasta, cooked al dente and drained

Chopped parsley

Sauté shrimp, scallops and fish in olive oil until slightly golden; do not overcook. Remove seafood and cover to keep warm.

In the same pan, sauté green onions and garlic for 1 minute. Add vermouth and tomatoes. Cook to reduce sauce slightly.

Add cream and cheese. Season with red pepper flakes and mix well.

Add cooked seafood. Serve seafood sauce over drained pasta. Sprinkle with parsley and additional Parmesan.

Classically, Italians do not use cheese with seafood but we like it this way!

Spaghetti Bordelaise

½ cup chopped green onions

½ cup olive oil

8 cloves garlic, minced

2 tablespoons white wine or dry vermouth

¾ teaspoon dried basil

½ teaspoon dried oregano

½ teaspoon dried thyme

½ teaspoon salt

¼ teaspoon freshly ground black pepper

3 tablespoons butter

½ cup chopped fresh parsley, plus extra for topping

1 pound dry spaghetti, cooked al dente and drained

1 cup Parmesan cheese

Sauté green onions in olive oil for about 2 minutes. Add garlic and mix well. Add wine, basil, oregano, thyme, salt, pepper, butter and parsley and cook 2 minutes longer.

Toss wine sauce with drained spaghetti. Place in a large serving bowl and coat with cheese.

Arrange chicken. Sprinkle extra parsley on top.

Except for cooking spaghetti at the last minute, the remaining recipe can be done several hours ahead.

Tomato Vodka Sauce on Rigatoni

SERVES 4

This is one of Libbie's specialties – we love it!

4 tablespoons butter

1 small onion, chopped

3 cloves garlic, minced

1 tablespoon dry Italian seasoning

2 cups chopped tomatoes, including juices

3 ounces prosciutto

½ cup vodka

¾ cup heavy cream

½ cup Parmigiano-Reggiano cheese, plus extra for on the side

Salt and pepper to taste

12 ounces rigatoni pasta, cooked al dente and drained

Melt butter in a skillet. Add onion and sauté until softened. Mix in garlic and Italian seasoning.

Add tomatoes and prosciutto and simmer 10 minutes. Add vodka and simmer 5 minutes. Add cream and cheese and simmer 4 minutes. Season with salt and pepper.

Add drained pasta to sauce. Serve with additional cheese on the side.

Tortellini with Gorgonzola

SERVES 4

Not so lean tortellini, but oh so good! Great first course.

TOPPING

½ cup dry white bread crumbs

1 tablespoon Parmigiano-Reggiano cheese

1 tablespoon olive oil

½ teaspoon dried oregano, crumbled

½ teaspoon dried basil, crumbled

SAUCE

2 cups heavy cream

4 ounces Gorgonzola cheese, crumbled

¼ teaspoon ground nutmeg

1 pound cheese tortellini

Mix all topping ingredients and set aside.

For sauce, simmer cream, Gorgonzola and nutmeg over medium heat, stirring until cheese melts. Cook 10 minutes or until mixture is reduced and is of a sauce consistency, stirring frequently.

Meanwhile, cook tortellini until just tender; drain thoroughly. Add tortellini to sauce and stir until heated through.

Preheat broiler.

Transfer pasta and sauce mixture to a large shallow broiler-proof baking dish. Sprinkle crumb topping over pasta to cover lightly.

Broil until top is lightly toasted; do not leave the broiler for even a minute!

Divide among plates and serve.

Veal and Tomato Cream Sauce over Penne

SERVES 4

It's snowing, it's raining, it's blowing – there is lightning and thunder – the fire is blazing, the wine is poured, there is love everywhere but most especially in our own little snug Paradise. But, we must dine before settling down for a long winter's night!

1 pound ground veal

1 bunch green onions, chopped

1 tablespoon olive oil

2 (14½-ounce) cans diced tomatoes, undrained

1 cup heavy cream

½ cup dry white wine

1 tablespoon tomato paste

12 ounces penne pasta, freshly cooked and drained

Salt and pepper to taste

Grated Parmigiano-Reggiano cheese

Sauté veal and green onions in olive oil until cooked through, breaking up veal with a spoon. Add tomatoes with their liquid, cream, wine and tomato paste. Simmer 45 minutes or until sauce thickens.

Toss drained pasta with sauce for 2 minutes. Season with salt and pepper. Serve, passing the Parmesan on the side.

Good night!

Keepers
NOTES

Baked Polenta with Garlic

Easiest and the best! This recipe is quite versatile – can be made ahead and served as is. Another time, layer with rich meat sauce or top with a mélange of sautéed wild mushrooms. Cut into rounds or squares and top with a creamy Gorgonzola sauce and bake. Try cutting into small dumplings and simmer in chicken broth. Perfect with Osso Buco (page 137). Soul Food.

2¾ cups chicken broth
2 cups water
1½ cups milk
3 cloves garlic, minced
2 teaspoons chopped rosemary
½ teaspoon salt
1½ cups polenta
4 tablespoons butter
6 tablespoons Parmigiano-
  Reggiano cheese, divided
Black pepper to taste

Preheat oven to 375 degrees.

Combine broth, water, milk, garlic, rosemary and salt in a saucepan. Bring to a boil. Gradually add polenta, stirring all the while. Reduce heat and cook 12 minutes. Add butter and 4 tablespoons cheese. Season with pepper.

Transfer mixture to a greased 9x11-inch baking dish. Sprinkle with remaining 2 tablespoons cheese.

Bake 30 minutes or until heated through and golden on top.

Polenta can be made ahead and baked when needed.

Baked Vegetable Risotto

Not the classic method but the result is perfectly delicious.

½ **pound shiitake mushrooms, thinly sliced**

2 **carrots, finely diced**

2 **tablespoons olive oil**

Salt and pepper to taste

¾ **pound broccoli, finely diced**

1 **red bell pepper, finely diced**

2 **tablespoons butter**

1 **shallot, minced**

1 **cup Arborio rice**

2 **cups chicken broth**

¼ **cup Parmesan cheese**

1 **cup panko**

Preheat oven to 350 degrees.

Sauté mushrooms and carrot in olive oil for 5 minutes. Season with salt and pepper and set aside.

In same pan, add broccoli and bell pepper and cook 2 minutes. Add to carrot mixture.

Melt butter in same pan. Add shallot and sauté 2 minutes. Add rice and cook 1 minute or until slightly golden. Add chicken broth and bring to a boil. Add cheese. Cover and cook, undisturbed, for 17 minutes.

Stir rice mixture and panko into sautéed vegetables. Correct seasoning if necessary. Transfer risotto to a greased baking dish.

Bake 45 minutes. Remove from oven and let stand 10 minutes before serving.

Company Rice

This truly was my "company rice" dish in the ol' days – it was quite "gourmet" then and we all loved it and still do!

1 large onion, minced
1 stick butter
1 cup sliced mushrooms
1 cup sliced almonds
1¾ cups dry rice
¾ cup grated Cheddar cheese
2 (10¾-ounce) cans consommé

Preheat oven to 350 degrees.

Sauté onion in butter until golden. Add mushrooms and almonds and cook 3 minutes. Mix sautéed mixture with rice, cheese and consommé. Mix well and transfer to a covered casserole dish. Bake 1 hour. Remove cover and bake 15 minutes longer.

Curried Rice

SERVES 4

This recipe is perfect as a side for any curry dish.

1 small yellow onion, chopped
3 tablespoons butter
1 teaspoon curry powder
1 cup rice
1¼ cups chicken broth
1¼ cups water

Sauté onion in butter for 5 minutes or until softened. Stir in curry powder and rice and cook until rice is opaque.

Add broth and water and bring to a boil. Cover and cook 20 minutes or until tender.

Corn Polenta with Tomato Mushroom Sauce

POLENTA

1 cup yellow cornmeal

1 cup water

2 cups chicken broth

1 cup fresh or frozen corn

8 tablespoons Parmigiano-
Reggiano cheese, divided

3 teaspoons olive oil, divided

TOMATO MUSHROOM SAUCE

2 teaspoons olive oil

1 onion, chopped

1 clove garlic, minced

1 teaspoon dried basil

½ teaspoon dried oregano

Pinch of dried red pepper flakes

8 ounces mushrooms, thinly sliced

½ cup dry white wine, divided

1 (14½-ounce) can diced tomatoes

Salt and pepper to taste

3 tablespoons chopped fresh
parsley

Whisk cornmeal and water in a small bowl to blend. Bring broth to a boil in a heavy saucepan and add cornmeal mixture all at once, stirring until mixture boils and thickens. Reduce heat. Add corn and simmer 15 minutes or until thickened, stirring often. Mix in 5 tablespoons cheese. Spoon polenta into an ungreased 9-inch diameter cake pan. Smooth top with a wet spatula. Cover and refrigerate. Bring polenta to room temperature before broiling.

For sauce, place oil in a heavy saucepan. Add onion and cook until tender. Add garlic, basil, oregano and pepper flakes and sauté 1 minute. Increase heat and add mushrooms. Sauté 2 minutes. Add ¼ cup wine and cook until liquid evaporates. Add remaining ¼ cup wine and tomatoes. Season with salt and pepper. Simmer sauce until reduced to 2½ cups.

Preheat broiler.

Turn out room temperature polenta onto a work surface, tapping on pan if necessary to release. Brush 1 teaspoon oil over polenta. Cut into 6 wedges. Place wedges, oil-side down, on a nonstick baking sheet. Brush top of polenta with remaining 2 teaspoons oil. Broil 3 minutes or until golden.

Meanwhile, bring sauce to simmer. Divide polenta among 6 plates. Spoon sauce over polenta and sprinkle with remaining 3 tablespoons cheese and chopped parsley.

Mushroom Sauce for Polenta

SERVES 6

4 tablespoons butter

1 onion, finely chopped

1 tablespoon minced fresh Italian parsley

1 clove garlic, minced

12 ounces mushrooms, thinly sliced, combination of fresh domestic and shiitake

1 ounce dried porcini, soaked in ¾ cup warm water, strain liquid and reserve

1½ cups chicken broth

1 tablespoon flour

2 tablespoons water

Salt and pepper to taste

Heat butter in a skillet. Add onion and sauté 2 minutes or until softened. Add parsley and garlic and mix. Add fresh mushrooms and porcini and sauté until lightly browned.

Add broth and reserved mushroom liquid and bring to boil. Reduce heat, cover and simmer 5 minutes.

Mix flour with 2 tablespoons water and stir into mushroom mixture. Cover and simmer, stirring occasionally, for about 10 minutes. Season with salt and pepper.

Serve over soft polenta.

Polenta – Tidbits of Information

Very soft polenta	6 parts liquid/1 part cornmeal	Plain or with topping
Soft polenta	5 parts liquid/1 part cornmeal	As a bed for stews
Firm polenta	4 parts liquid/1 part cornmeal	As a bed for stews to cool and slice into wedges to fry or broil and serve with topping
Very firm polenta	3 to 3½ parts liquid/ 1 part cornmeal	Fry, broil or grill

Try to use a bag or box of cornmeal soon after you buy it. Store cornmeal in the freezer.

Rice Mexicana

SERVES 6

Somehow, learning to cook Mexican cuisine was never in my repertoire until we moved to the Valley where we celebrated Cinco de Mayo every year. We really got into the festivity, setting up tables around the pool, decorating and cooking for days. We did leave mixing the Margaritas until the last! This is our standby side dish when cooking anything Mexican.

1 large yellow onion, chopped
¼ cup vegetable oil
2 cups dry long grain rice
2 cloves garlic, minced
1 (14½-ounce) can diced tomatoes
4 cups canned beef bouillon
1½ teaspoons ground cumin

In a large skillet, cook onion in oil for 3 minutes or until soft. Add rice and cook another 3 minutes, stirring until rice is pale yellow. Add garlic and stir. Add tomatoes, bouillon and cumin and bring to a boil over high heat.

Reduce to low heat. Cover and simmer 20 minutes or until liquid is absorbed and rice is tender.

Saffron Rice

SERVES 8

A colorful dish to accompany scampi.

3 tablespoons unsalted butter
3 tablespoons olive oil
1 onion, chopped
2 cups dry long-grain rice
¼ teaspoon saffron threads, crushed
5 cups chicken broth
½ cup snipped fresh chives
Salt and pepper to taste

Melt butter with oil in a skillet. Add onion and sauté 5 minutes or until golden. Mix in rice and saffron. Add broth and bring to a boil.

Reduce heat to low. Cover and simmer 35 minutes or until all liquid is absorbed.

Mix in chives and season with salt and pepper.

Rice Pilaf with Pistachios and Golden Raisins

A winner!

1 large onion, chopped

1 teaspoon turmeric

½ teaspoon cardamom

6 tablespoons butter, divided

1⅔ cup dry rice

3½ cups chicken broth

½ cup pistachios

½ cup golden raisins, soaked in boiling water to cover for 1 minute and drained

½ cup thinly sliced green onions

Salt and pepper to taste

Sauté onion, turmeric and cardamom in 5 tablespoons butter over low heat, stirring until onion is softened.

Add rice and cook, stirring until rice is coated with butter.

Add broth and bring to a boil. Reduce heat, cover and simmer 17 minutes or until liquid is absorbed and the rice is tender.

Stir in pistachios, raisins, green onions and remaining tablespoon of butter. Season with salt and pepper.

Risotto with Porcini

SERVES 4

Who does not love risotto! Any kind, any time, anywhere! This method is a little different but the result is excellent. Keep a bag of dry porcini in the freezer – I truly believe they should be a staple in any kitchen.

¾ cup hot water

½ ounce dried porcini mushrooms

1½ tablespoons olive oil

3 tablespoons parsley, minced

2 green onions, chopped

1¼ cups dry Arborio rice

3 tablespoons dry white wine

3 cups chicken broth, divided

⅓ cup Parmigiano-Reggiano cheese

2 tablespoons unsalted butter

Black pepper to taste

Pour hot water over mushrooms and let stand 30 minutes to soften. Remove mushrooms from liquid, reserving liquid. Strain soaking liquid through fine sieve and set aside. Chop mushrooms finely and set aside.

Heat olive oil in a saucepan over medium heat. Add parsley and green onions and sauté 3 minutes. Add mushrooms and sauté 5 minutes. Add rice and stir until opaque.

Add wine and cook and stir until no liquid remains. Add reserved mushroom liquid and 1½ cups broth and bring to a boil, stirring occasionally.

Add remaining 1½ cups broth and return to a boil. Cook over medium heat, stirring frequently, for about 15 minutes.

Remove from heat and mix in cheese and butter. Season with pepper. Cover and let stand 3 minutes.

Risotto 101

We all concede that Amy has "the touch" with her Risotto – rich chicken broth, careful, slow stirring, cooking stopped at just the right moment, served immediately on a beautiful Italian plate, a generous sprinkling of Parmigiano-Reggiano and a sparkling smile!

3 tablespoons extra virgin olive oil

1 medium-size yellow onion, finely diced

2 cups dry Arborio rice

½ cup dry white wine

3½ cups chicken broth, heated

4 tablespoons unsalted butter

½ cup Parmigiano-Reggiano cheese, plus extra for sprinkling

In a large, deep skillet, heat olive oil. Add onion and cook slowly and gently until softened, making sure the onion is cooked through but not browned. Taking time here is an important step.

Add rice and stir with a wooden spoon for 3 to 4 minutes. Add wine and cook several minutes.

Add warm chicken broth, a ladle full at a time, stirring until absorbed. Continue until all broth has been incorporated, stirring all the while. Cook until rice is a little al dente and rice is only slightly wet. This should take about 15 minutes in all.

Stir in butter and cheese and mix well. Serve ASAP! Pass extra Parmigiano-Reggiano.

Risotto Murray

SERVES 6

Cindy and Lyndon blessed us with this divine risotto at lunch one day. There we sat, in their beautiful Belvedere home, looking across the Bay to San Francisco, visiting with dear friends, loving every minute, every morsel, every sip! The preparation of this risotto does allow the hosts to step away from the stove. This is superb!

3 cups chicken broth

2 tablespoons butter

½ cup chopped yellow onion

1½ cups dry Arborio rice

3 tablespoons olive oil

3 green onions, chopped

⅓ cup coarsely grated zucchini

⅓ cup coarsely grated carrot

2 cups chopped fresh spinach

3 tomatoes, diced

1 ounce dried porcini mushrooms, rinsed, not soaked

1 teaspoons dried basil

¼ cup heavy cream

¼ cup dry white wine

¾ cup Parmigiano-Reggiano cheese, plus extra for serving

Salt and pepper to taste

Heat broth to a boil.

Melt butter in a large skillet. Add onion and sauté until softened. Add rice and cook until rice is lightly golden. Add 1½ cups boiling broth and cover. Cook 10 minutes.

In a separate skillet, heat olive oil. Add green onions, zucchini, carrot, spinach, tomato and mushrooms and cook 7 to 8 minutes or until vegetables softened.

Add remaining 1½ cups broth along with sautéed vegetables to rice. Stir in basil, cream and wine and simmer 10 minutes, stirring frequently to prevent sticking.

Mix in cheese and season with salt and pepper. Pass extra cheese on the side.

Sausage and Spinach Risotto

Have you ever met a risotto you didn't like! This is one you will love!

4 mild Italian sausages, casings removed

2 cloves garlic, finely chopped

4-5 cups chicken broth

1 large yellow onion, finely chopped

2 tablespoons olive oil

2 cups dry Arborio rice

½ cup red wine

1 pound fresh spinach, chopped

2 tablespoons butter

½ cup Parmigiano-Reggiano cheese

Crumble sausage into a skillet and sauté 3 minutes. Add garlic and cook 1 to 2 minutes; set aside.

Heat broth in a separate pot.

In a large skillet, sauté onion in olive oil for 3 to 4 minutes or until light golden. Stir in rice. Add wine and stir until wine is absorbed. Add 2 cups broth and cook 8 to 10 minutes.

Add remaining broth, ½ cup at a time, and cook 10 minutes longer, stirring all the while. The rice should be slightly al dente.

Mix in cooked sausage and spinach. Add butter and cheese.

Rich, delicious.

Seafood Risotto

SERVES 6

I order this risotto whenever I go Kuleto's in downtown San Francisco. This is as close as I can get in attempting to duplicate their dish – I think I am there!

2½ cups water

2 (8-ounce) bottles clam juice

6 tablespoons olive oil, divided

3 shallots, finely chopped

1½ cups dry Arborio rice

½ cup white wine

1 pinch saffron

1 (14½-ounce) can diced tomatoes

1 pound raw prawns, peeled, deveined and coarsely chopped

¾ pound bay scallops, blotted dry

3 cloves garlic, minced

Salt and pepper to taste

1 tablespoon finely chopped fresh parsley

Combine water and clam juice in a saucepan and bring to a simmer; keep warm.

Heat 3 tablespoons oil in a heavy saucepan. Add shallots and sauté until golden. Add rice and sauté 2 minutes. Add wine and stir until liquid is absorbed. Add saffron and tomatoes and cook until liquid is absorbed.

Add 1 cup clam juice mixture to rice and simmer until liquid is absorbed, stirring often. Continue adding clam juice mixture, ½ cup at a time, until rice is tender but slightly firm in center and mixture is creamy.

Heat remaining 3 tablespoons oil in a separate heavy skillet. Add shrimp, scallops and garlic and sauté 6 minutes or until seafood is opaque.

Mix seafood into rice and cook 3 minutes longer. Remove from heat. Season with salt and pepper. Transfer to a bowl and stir in chopped parsley.

Soft Polenta

SERVES 6

There are times a savory stew requires soft polenta on the side – this is it!

1 onion, finely chopped
2 tablespoons olive oil
3 cloves garlic, minced
4½ cups chicken broth
1½ cups water
1½ cups dry polenta
4 tablespoons unsalted butter
1 teaspoon dried thyme
½ cup Parmesan cheese

Sauté onion in olive oil until softened. Add garlic and cook 1 minute. Add broth and water. Slowly whisk in polenta, mixing constantly. Cook about 25 minutes, stirring often.

Add butter, thyme and cheese. Serve immediately or keep soft by placing in a metal bowl set over warm, simmering water.

Wild Rice, Barley and Mushrooms

A great combination.

1¼ cups dry wild rice
3 cups water
6 green onions, white and some of green, sliced
1 stick butter, divided
2 tablespoons barley
3 (11-ounce) cans bouillon soup
1 teaspoon fresh or dried thyme
8 ounces mushrooms, sliced

Cook wild rice in water 50 minutes or until tender; drain.

Preheat oven to 350 degrees.

Sauté green onions in 4 tablespoons butter until tender. Add barley, cooked rice, bouillon and thyme.

Transfer to a casserole dish and cover tightly. Bake 1 hour.

Meanwhile, sauté mushrooms in remaining 4 tablespoons butter; set aside. When rice is done baking, stir in sautéed mushrooms.

A Wild and Wonderful Rice Casserole

SERVES 10

*My dear niece, Kathy, served this on a buffet table many years ago.
It was a hit then and now! We once multiplied the recipe 20 times and
served 300 guests at a fundraiser! Everyone wanted the recipe!*

2 (6-ounce) packages long-grain
   and wild rice mix

1 stick butter

1 medium onion, chopped

⅔ cup flour

Black pepper to taste

2 cups half-and-half

2 cups chicken broth

⅔ cup chopped fresh parsley

1 cup sliced or chopped almonds

Preheat oven to 425 degrees.

Prepare rice mix according to package directions, decreasing cooking time by 5 minutes.

Melt butter in a large skillet. Add onion and cook over low heat until tender, but not brown. Stir in flour and pepper. Gradually stir in half-and-half and broth and cook and stir until thickened. Add parsley, almonds and cooked rice.

Transfer mixture to a 4-quart casserole dish. Bake, uncovered, for 30 minutes.

*Four cups cubed cooked chicken or turkey can be added along with the parsley and almonds. One medium fryer, simmered until tender, will produce just about
4 cups chopped chicken and the broth necessary for this recipe.*

Almond Torte

An old favorite! I made this so often in the 60's – it was delicious then and it still is now. The almond and meringue are on the top and bottom of the cake.

1 stick butter, softened
½ cup sugar
4 egg yolks
1 cup flour
1 teaspoon baking powder
⅛ teaspoon salt
1½ tablespoons evaporated milk
1½ tablespoons water
½ teaspoon vanilla

MERINGUE
4 egg whites
¾ cup plus 1 tablespoon sugar, divided
½ cup sliced almonds
½ teaspoon cinnamon

CREAM FILLING
½ cup sugar
2 tablespoons cornstarch
1 egg, unbeaten
2 cups evaporated milk
1 teaspoon almond extract

Preheat oven to 325 degrees.

Cream butter until fluffy. Add sugar gradually and beat until creamy. Add egg yolks, beating well.

In a separate bowl, mix flour, baking powder and salt. Combine milk and water and add alternately with dry ingredients to batter, beginning and ending with flour. Add vanilla. Pour batter into 2 greased 9-inch cake pans.

For meringue, beat egg whites until stiff. Gradually beat in ¾ cup sugar. Spread meringue over unbaked batter. Sprinkle almonds on top. Combine cinnamon and remaining 1 tablespoon sugar and sprinkle over almonds.

Bake 30 to 35 minutes. When cool, spread cream filling between layers, meringue-side up. To make filling, blend sugar and cornstarch in the top of a double boiler. Add egg and stir until well blended. Add milk slowly and cook, stirring constantly, over boiling water for 10 minutes or until thickened. Add almond extract.

Almond Fudge Torte

SERVES 10

I believe this is the best cake I have ever made! Serve thin wedges – it is rich!

1 teaspoon instant coffee granules

2 tablespoons hot water

4 ounces semi-sweet chocolate, melted

3 eggs, separated

1 stick butter, softened

¾ cup sugar

2 ounces almond paste, crumbled

½ cup flour

Chocolate Glaze (recipe below)

Preheat oven to 350 degrees.

Dissolve coffee in hot water. Stir in melted chocolate.

Beat egg whites until stiff.

In another bowl, beat butter and sugar until fluffy. Add almond paste and blend until smooth. Mix in egg yolks, melted chocolate mixture and flour.

Fold in beaten egg whites, about one-third at a time until just blended. Spread batter in a greased and cocoa-dusted 8-inch round cake pan.

Bake 30 minutes; do not overbake. Watch carefully if your oven runs hot.

Cool on a rack about 20 minutes. Turn out of pan to cool thoroughly.

Spread with Chocolate Glaze. Let stand 2 to 4 hours or until glaze hardens. If refrigerated, bring to room temperature before serving.

CHOCOLATE GLAZE

4 ounces semi-sweet chocolate, cut into small chunks

1 tablespoon solid shortening

Combine chocolate with shortening in the top of a double boiler. Stir over simmering water until chocolate is just melted. Remove from heat and cool, stirring occasionally. Glaze should be slightly thickened to spread over cake.

Chocolate Heaven!

The Best Cheesecake

Really! A friend parted with this recipe years ago after much pleading. And now, a cast of thousands can produce The Best Cheesecake – Really!

4 (8-ounce) containers whipped cream cheese (do not substitute), room temperature

1 stick butter, room temperature

16 ounces sour cream, room temperature

2 tablespoons cornstarch

1 teaspoon vanilla

1 teaspoon fresh lemon juice

1½ cups sugar

4 eggs

1 (10-ounce) package sweetened frozen raspberries, thawed

Preheat oven to 375 degrees.

Combine cream cheese, butter, sour cream, cornstarch, vanilla, lemon juice and sugar in a food processor or with an electric mixer. (The mixer produces a fluffier cake, but either way is satisfactory.)

Beat in eggs, one at a time, mixing well after each addition.

Grease a 9½-inch springform pan and wrap the outside of the pan with 2 layers of foil. Pour batter into prepared pan. Place pan in a larger pan filled one-third full with hot water.

Bake 1 hour, 20 minutes. The top surface will be quite gold brown. Remove carefully to a rack to cool. Refrigerate until chilled.

Blend raspberries in food processor and press through strainer to remove seeds.

To serve, place a small amount of raspberry sauce on each plate and top with small slice of The Best Cheesecake – Really!

The Best Caramel Custard

Amy's specialty – it truly is the best caramel custard! It's a process, but worth it. Prepare several days ahead and refrigerate.

⅔ cup sugar, divided
½ teaspoon cream of tartar
2 cups heavy cream
1 (2-inch) piece of vanilla bean, or
    1 tablespoon vanilla
¼ cup sugar
5 egg yolks
1 tablespoon Kahlúa liqueur

Preheat oven to 325 degrees. Place a nonstick loaf pan in oven on a baking sheet.

Combine ⅓ cup sugar and cream of tartar in a heavy small saucepan. Pour in just enough water to cover. Cook over medium-low heat until sugar melts, shaking pan occasionally. Decrease heat to low and cook, without stirring, until sugar caramelizes and turns a gold mahogany brown. Quickly pour hot caramel into a heated mold and swirl until bottom and sides of mold are evenly coated with caramel. Turn upside down on a baking sheet.

Place cream, vanilla and remaining ⅓ cup sugar in a heavy saucepan. Cook over low heat until cream is scalded; watching carefully.

Gently whisk together egg yolks and Kahlúa in a mixing bowl. Slowly pour in scalded cream. Gently strain mixture through a sieve into caramelized mold. Let stand several seconds, then skim off any foam.

Set mold into larger pan filled with enough hot water to come two-thirds up the sides of the mold.

Bake 50 to 60 minutes or until a knife inserted in the edge of the custard comes

THE BEST CARAMEL CUSTARD — CONTINUED

out with a thick curd-like coating. Remove from oven and carefully lift from water bath. Place a piece of plastic wrap directly on surface of custard so a skin does not form. Cool at room temperature, then refrigerate at least 6 hours or, preferably, up to several days.

Unmold custard just before serving. Place empty mold in a pan of hot water to dissolve remaining caramel and pour over custard. Slice and serve.

The Best Pound Cake

This is it! Look no further – using the cream cheese and cake flour creates a delectably tender pound cake.

1 (8-ounce) package cream cheese, softened

1½ sticks butter, softened

1½ cups granulated sugar

1½ teaspoons vanilla (may substitute 1½ teaspoons lemon juice, 1 teaspoon vanilla and 1 teaspoon grated lemon zest)

2 eggs

2 cups sifted cake flour (do not use unbleached flour)

1½ teaspoons baking powder

Powdered sugar, optional

Preheat oven to 325 degrees.

Whip cream cheese with butter until fluffy. Add sugar and vanilla and mix until light and fluffy. Add eggs and beat until blended.

Mix flour and baking powder and blend into batter at low speed. Pour batter into a greased and floured 9x5-inch loaf pan or Bundt pan.

Bake 1 hour, 10 minutes. Cool 5 minutes. Remove from pan and cool completely on a wire rack.

Sprinkle with sifted powdered sugar, if desired

Apple Crisp

This is the quickest, bestest apple dessert in existence!

8 apples, peeled and thinly sliced
2 tablespoons butter
Cinnamon
1 cup baking mix
1 cup sugar
1 egg

Preheat oven to 350 degrees.

Arrange apples in a 9-inch square baking dish. Dot with butter and sprinkle with cinnamon.

Combine baking mix, sugar and egg in a small bowl. With a fork, blend together keeping mixture as crumbly as possible. Sprinkle mixture evenly over the apples.

Bake about 45 minutes. Remove from oven and serve warm or cold.

Yum for breakfast!

Bonet Libbie

Our family's Christmas tradition – any day of the year would be a holiday when serving this spectacular dessert.

1 quart milk

1½ cups sugar, divided

6 tablespoons ground chocolate

6 tablespoons cocoa powder

8 eggs, beaten

1 teaspoon vanilla

½ cup brandy

½ cup rum

16 Amaretti macaroons, use more
   if cookies are small

1 cup chopped walnuts

Whipped cream for topping

Preheat oven to 350 degrees.

In a saucepan, combine milk, ¾ cup sugar, chocolate and cocoa. Heat until warm; do not boil. Mix well and remove from heat. Slowly add beaten eggs, vanilla, brandy, rum and macaroons. Blend well.

Melt remaining ¾ cup sugar in a saucepan until lightly caramelized, stirring constantly as the sugar melts. Pour sugar into a heavy, nonstick Bundt pan, making sure all surfaces are covered. Top with the walnuts. Pour in the chocolate mixture.

Set mold in a pan of hot water. Bake 1 hour. Cool on a rack and refrigerate overnight.

Unmold onto a large serving dish with sides since there is a generous amount of sauce. Serve with a dollop of whipped cream.

Chocolate Almond Paté

Sinfully fantastic – that is, if you love chocolate!

1¼ cups heavy cream
4 tablespoons unsalted butter
1 pound bittersweet chocolate, finely chopped
1 cup ground toasted almonds
1 teaspoon almond extract
Whipped cream and mint sprigs for garnish

Combine cream and butter in a saucepan and bring to a simmer. Reduce heat and stir in chocolate until melted and smooth. Immediately remove from heat and mix in almonds and almond extract.

Pour mixture into a 7½x3½x2½-inch loaf pan lined with wax paper. Cover and chill overnight.

Invert pan onto a work surface. Peel off wax paper and cut into thin slices. Decorate each slice with a dollop of whipped cream and a mint sprig.

English Fruitcake

My Swiss friend's English husband's mother gave me this recipe many years ago and it is still one of our favorites.

2½ cups all-purpose flour
1 teaspoon baking powder
⅔ cup golden raisins or mixed glazed fruit
2 sticks butter, softened
1¼ cups sugar
2 eggs
⅔ cup milk

Preheat oven to 325 degrees.

Sift flour with baking powder. Mix in raisins; set aside.

Beat butter and sugar until light and fluffy. Add eggs, one at a time, beating thoroughly after each addition. Add dry ingredients, a little at a time, beating well after each addition. Add milk and mix well. Pour batter into a 9x5-inch loaf pan, or 3 small loaf pans.

Bake 1 hour, 20 minutes for the large pan, or 1 hour for the small. Cool on a rack.

Chocolate Amaretti Cake

Any dessert made with Amaretti cookies is hard to beat. Moist and deeply full-flavored. Winner! Winner!

Butter flavored nonstick cooking spray

¾ **cup chopped bittersweet chocolate or semi-sweet chocolate chips**

1 **cup slivered almonds**

1 **cup baby Amaretti cookies (about 2 ounces)**

1 **stick unsalted butter, room temperature**

⅔ **cup sugar**

2 **teaspoons orange zest**

4 **large eggs**

Unsweetened cocoa powder or powdered sugar for sifting

Preheat oven to 350 degrees.

Spray a 9-inch springform with the nonstick spray and refrigerate.

Microwave chocolate until melted and smooth, stirring every 20 seconds.

Combine almonds and cookies in a food processor and pulse until finely ground. Transfer to a bowl.

Add butter and sugar to food processor and blend until creamy. Add orange zest. Add eggs, one at a time, and blend until incorporated.

Clean the sides of the processor bowl. Add nut mixture and melted chocolate and pulse until blended. Pour batter into prepared pan.

Bake 30 to 35 minutes or until the center puffs and a tester inserted into the center of the cake comes out clean. Cool in pan 15 minutes.

Transfer to a platter. Sift with cocoa powder or powdered sugar and serve.

Chocolate Crunch Cake

An old recipe – a new twist.

⅔ cup chopped walnuts

1 stick butter, melted

½ cup sugar

⅔ cup bread crumbs

1 (18-ounce) package devil's food
  cake mix

1 cup heavy cream, whipped and
  sweetened

Preheat oven to 350 degrees.

Combine walnuts, butter, sugar and crumbs and mix well with fork. Divide mixture between 2 ungreased cake pans. Press down firmly.

Prepare cake according to directions on the package. Pour over crumb mixture in pans.

Bake 25 to 30 minutes. Cool in pans 10 to 15 minutes. Remove and cool completely on racks.

To assemble, place one layer, crunch-side down, on a platter. Spread with half of the whipped cream. Place second layer over cream, crunch-side up.

Top with dollops of whipped cream placed around the edge of the cake and a dollop in the center.

Chocolate Mousse Pie

One of my oldest chocolate dessert recipes – one of my best.

CRUST

1½ (12-ounce) packages plain
  chocolate wafers

1½ sticks butter, melted

FILLING

½ cup sugar

⅔ cup water

1 (12-ounce) package chocolate
  chips

3 tablespoons dark rum

2 tablespoons milk

6 egg yolks

¼ teaspoon almond extract

3 cups heavy cream, whipped

Whipped cream for piping

Chocolate leaves, fresh
  raspberries, holly or candied
  orange peel for garnish

Process cookies with melted butter and press into the bottom and up the sides of a greased 9-inch springform pan.

For filling, combine sugar and water in a small saucepan. Bring to a boil and cook 3 minutes.

Grind chocolate chips in a food processor. With motor on, gradually pour in hot sugar syrup, rum, milk, egg yolks and almond extract. Allow to cool.

Fold whipped cream into cooled mixture. Pour over crust and chill for at least 6 hours.

To serve, remove sides of pan. Pipe whipped cream around border and decorate with garnish of your choice.

Chocolate and Walnut Tart

Easily doubled or tripled with an adjustment in baking pan size. Putting this together could not be simpler and the result could not be better.

TART CRUST
1 stick butter
1 cup flour
1 tablespoon sugar
1 tablespoon vanilla
1½ teaspoons water

FILLING
2 eggs
1 cup sugar
½ cup flour
1 stick butter, melted
1 cup chocolate chips
1 tablespoon bourbon
1 teaspoon vanilla
1 cup chopped walnuts
Whipped cream

Preheat oven to 350 degrees.

Place butter, flour and sugar in a food processor and pulse until crumbly. Mix vanilla with water and gradually add to mixture in processor, taking care not to overmix. Press crust evenly into tart shell.

For filling, combine eggs, sugar, flour, butter, chocolate, bourbon and vanilla in a food processor. Pulse until mixed. Add walnuts and pulse, taking care not to overmix; walnuts should remain chunky.

Turn mixture into unbaked tart shell. Bake 35 to 40 minutes or until golden brown.

Pass whipped cream separately.

Cinnamon Apple Cake

Bill's favorite!

BATTER

1½ cups flour

2 teaspoons baking powder

½ teaspoon salt

4 tablespoons butter, softened

¾ cup sugar

¼ teaspoon cinnamon

1 egg

½ cup milk

TOPPING

2 apples, peeled and cut into
¼-inch slices

¾ teaspoon cinnamon

2 tablespoons sugar

2 tablespoons butter

Preheat oven to 375 degrees.

Sift together flour, baking powder and salt. In a separate bowl, cream butter with sugar and cinnamon until fluffy. Beat in egg. Add dry ingredients alternately with milk. Spread batter into a greased 9x9x2-inch cake pan.

Arrange apple slices symmetrically over batter. Combine cinnamon and sugar and sprinkle over apples. Dot with butter.

Bake 40 minutes. Serve warm. Especially delicious for breakfast.

Dutch Cinnamon Apple Cake

Everyone's absolute favorite – many years later Amy and Bill have confessed they have made and consumed the entire cake, not leaving a tell-tale crumb behind!

BATTER

1½ cups flour

2 teaspoons baking powder

½ teaspoon salt

5 tablespoons butter, softened

¾ cup sugar

¼ teaspoon cinnamon

1 egg

½ cup milk

TOPPING

3-4 apples, peeled and cut into ¼-inch slices

1 teaspoon cinnamon

3 tablespoons sugar

3 tablespoons butter

Preheat oven to 375 degrees.

Sift together flour, baking powder and salt; set aside. Cream butter with sugar and cinnamon until light and fluffy. Beat in egg. Add dry ingredients alternately with milk. Spread batter evenly in a greased 9x12-inch rimmed baking sheet.

Arrange apple slices over batter in even rows. Combine cinnamon and sugar and sprinkle over apples. Dot with butter.

Bake 40 minutes. Serve warm. Especially delicious for breakfast.

Fresh Fruit with Creamy Grand Marnier Sauce

SERVES 8

This is one of those "perfect, every time" desserts.

1 (8-ounce) package cream cheese, softened

1 cup sour cream

½ cup plus 6 tablespoons powdered sugar

½ cup heavy cream

3 tablespoons Grand Marnier or other orange-flavored liqueur

8 cups assorted fruit, such as grapes, strawberries, raspberries and blueberries, or fresh pineapple, blueberries, oranges, bananas and grapes

Mint leaves for garnish

Combine cream cheese, sour cream, powdered sugar and heavy cream. Mix in Grand Marnier. Transfer sauce to a bowl and refrigerate 1 hour, or up to 1 day.

To serve, divide fruit among 8 stemmed glasses. Top with sauce. Decorate with mint leaves.

Fruit and Cheese

Very pretty, very good.

¼ **cup red port**
1 **tablespoon sugar**
½ **cup water**
½ **cup dried cherries**
3 **ripe Bosc pears**
1½ **cups crumbled Stilton cheese
(5 ounces)**

In a saucepan, bring port, sugar and water to a boil over medium-high heat, watching all the while. Remove from heat and add cherries. Set aside at least 2 hours or overnight.

Strain the cherries and return liquid to high heat. Reduce heat and simmer 5 minutes or until slightly reduced. Remove from heat and stir in cherries.

Quarter pears lengthwise and core. Thinly slice each quarter lengthwise, leaving slices attached at stem end. Fan out 2 pear quarters on each plate.

Spoon about 1½ tablespoons of cherries and sauce over each serving. Sprinkle each with ¼ cup of cheese.

Grapefruit Sorbet

Bursting with flavor!

2½ **cups fresh grapefruit juice**
1 **cup Simple Syrup (recipe below)**
½ **cup fresh lemon juice**
⅓ **cup tequila**

Combine all ingredients. Freeze in an ice cream maker according to manufacturer's directions.

SIMPLE SYRUP
2 **cups sugar**
1 **cup water**

Combine sugar and water and cook for 5 minutes. Cool.

Girdle Buster

This is Benita's fault – many girdles have been busted since she shared this recipe!

20 chocolate wafer sandwich
   cookies, crushed
4 tablespoons butter, melted
1 quart coffee ice cream
Chocolate Sauce (recipe below)
Toasted Almonds (recipe below)

Mix cookie crumbs with butter and press into a 9-inch pie pan. Freeze.

Spoon ice cream into shell and refreeze.

Serve generous slices topped with Chocolate Sauce and Toasted Almonds.

CHOCOLATE SAUCE
1 (5-ounce) can evaporated milk
2 tablespoons butter
½ cup sugar
1 (1-ounce) square bitter chocolate
½ (12-ounce) package chocolate
   bits
½ teaspoon vanilla

Combine all sauce ingredients in a saucepan. Cook over low heat until chocolate is melted and slightly thickened.

TOASTED ALMONDS
4 tablespoons butter
Almonds

Melt butter in a pan. Add almonds and cook until lightly browned.

Grasshopper Pie

The 1960's favorite pie – those were the days that a company dinner ended with sweet liquors which seems to have fallen out of favor in the 2000's, but not this old timer!

CRUST
2 tablespoons butter, melted
14 chocolate wafer sandwich
   cookies, crushed

FILLING
24 marshmallows
½ cup milk
4 tablespoons green
   crème de mint
2 tablespoons white
   crème de cocoa
1 cup heavy cream, whipped

Mix butter and cookie crumbs in a bowl. Press mixture into a 9-inch pie pan; set aside.

For filling, combine marshmallows and milk in a medium saucepan. Simmer, stirring constantly, until marshmallows are melted. Mix in crème de mint and crème de cocoa.

Fold in whipped cream. Pour filling into crust and freeze. Serve frozen.

Peanut Butter Pie

The horseback riding was great and the camp cooks knew what they were doing and I knew what I was doing when I asked for the recipe! Easy.

1 (8-ounce) package cream cheese,
   softened
¼ cup crunchy peanut butter
1 cup powdered sugar
1 (16-ounce) container frozen
   whipped topping, thawed
1 graham cracker crust, baked

Whip cream cheese until fluffy. Fold in peanut butter, sugar and whipped topping.

Spoon mixture into crust. Chill several hours. Needs no further embellishment.

Lemon Cream Cake

Celebrate for any occasion with this lovely cake. This is one of my much-loved recipes.

1 (18-ounce) package white cake mix
1 (3-ounce) package lemon pudding and pie filling (not instant)
1 cup heavy cream, whipped
1 cup shredded coconut, toasted

Prepare cake according to package directions. Cool layers and split each layer horizontally in half.

In the meantime, make the lemon pie filling according to package directions. Cool completely.

Fold whipped cream into cooled pie filling.

To assemble, spread filling over each cake layer. Stack layers. Spread filling over the top and around the sides. Sprinkle cake with toasted coconut. Cover and refrigerate overnight.

Lemon Ginger Pie

This is a very refreshing dessert and greatly appreciated by ginger lovers.

1 store-bought pie crust

FILLING
1 ounce fresh ginger, peeled and
　finely chopped
1 cup plus 3 tablespoons sugar
2 cups fresh lemon juice
1 cup water
¼ cup cornstarch
3 egg yolks

MERINGUE
3 egg whites
⅓ cup sugar
¼ teaspoon vanilla

Bake pie crust according to package directions; set aside.

To make filling, finely chop ginger with sugar in a food processor until well blended. Transfer to a saucepan and add lemon juice and water. Bring to a boil and cook until sugar dissolves. Remove from heat and steep 1 hour.

Mix cornstarch with egg yolks and add to the cooled ginger mixture. Cook until thickened, stirring all the while. Remove from heat, cover and cool about 3 hours. (I hurry this along by placing in the freezer until cool.)

Preheat oven to 400 degrees.

For meringue, beat egg whites until foamy. Slowly add sugar and beat until stiff. Add vanilla.

Spoon filling into pie shell to the edges. Top with meringue. Bake 5 minutes or until meringue is nicely tan, watching carefully.

Mocha Chocolate Icebox Cake

This dessert gets the Oscar! I have been "throwing" it together for years, never measuring an ingredient, but Amy insisted we get this down in black and white!

This has always been her birthday request.

1½ packages ladyfingers

1 (8-ounce) package cream cheese

½ cup brown sugar

1 heaping teaspoon coffee
   granules

12 marshmallows

1 (12-ounce) package chocolate
   chips

½ cup milk

4 egg yolks, beaten

1 (¼-ounce) envelope unflavored
   gelatin

¼ cup warm water

1 teaspoon vanilla

4 egg whites

Pinch of salt

1 cup heavy cream, whipped

Line a 10-inch springform pan with ladyfingers.

In a food processor, blend cream cheese, brown sugar and coffee granules. Transfer to a large bowl; set aside.

Melt marshmallows and chocolate chips with milk in a pan over a double boiler. Add egg yolks and mix well. Mix gelatin in warm water and add to the chocolate mixture. Stir in vanilla; set aside.

Add a pinch of salt to egg whites and beat until soft peaks form. Set aside.

Fold chocolate mixture into cream cheese until well blended. Gently fold in egg whites, then fold in whipped cream.

Pour mixture over ladyfingers in pan. Cover with foil and freeze. Remove from freezer 15 minutes before serving.

Oven Roasted Pears with Warm Blue Cheese

Easy finale with a small glass of sweet wine on the side.

3 ripe, but firm, red Anjou or Bosc pears

1 lemon, halved

1 tablespoon butter

1 tablespoon sugar

1 ounce blue cheese, such as Maytag, Point Reyes Original or Gorgonzola

½ cup chopped toasted walnuts

Preheat oven to 400 degrees.

For each pear, cut in half lengthwise, leaving the stem intact on one half. Using a melon baller, scoop out the seeds and the long fibers that run down the middle of each half. Rub the cut surface of pear with lemon halves and set aside on a plate, cut side-up. Squeeze juice from lemon halves over all the pears. This may be done up to 2 hours in advance.

Grease a baking dish with 1 tablespoon butter. Sprinkle sugar over the bottom of the dish. Place pears in dish, cut-side down.

Bake 35 minutes or until the sugar and butter melt to form a syrup, the cut surface of the pears begins to turn a little golden and the pears are cooked through. Turn the pears over and gently push them around in the syrup.

Transfer pears to individual plates. Place about 2 teaspoons of cheese in each pear cavity. Scatter walnuts over the pears, including a few on the plates. Let stand about 20 minutes before serving.

Peach Crisp

We are lucky! We have our very own peach farmer in the family! Tony's peaches are perfect and this dessert shows them off deliciously!

1 cup sugar

½ cup flour

½ cup granola

⅔ teaspoon cinnamon

⅔ teaspoon nutmeg

⅛ teaspoon salt

4 tablespoons butter

¼ cup orange juice

3 pounds peaches, peeled or unpeeled and sliced ¾-inch thick

Whipped cream or ice cream for topping

Preheat oven to 375 degrees.

Stir together sugar, flour, granola, cinnamon, nutmeg and salt. Blend in butter with your fingertips until mixtures forms small clumps.

Mix orange juice with peaches and spread in a 9x13-inch baking dish. Top with crumb mixture.

Bake 35 minutes. Serve warm with a dollop of whipped cream or vanilla ice cream. Leftovers are great for breakfast.

Pineapple Cake

ENOUGH FOR A CROWD.

Everything Janet cooks is perfection and this cake is an excellent example!

1 (18-ounce) package yellow cake mix

1 (20-ounce) can crushed pineapple, undrained

1 cup brown sugar

1 (6-ounce) package vanilla instant pudding

2½ cups milk

1 (16-ounce) container frozen whipped topping, thawed

Toasted coconut

Prepare cake mix according to directions on package.

In the meanwhile, cook undrained pineapple with brown sugar for 10 minutes.

When done baking, poke cake all over with the tines of a fork. Pour pineapple mixture over the top and cool.

Mix pudding with milk and allow to thicken. Spread pudding over pineapple. Cover cake with whipped topping and decorate with toasted coconut.

Plum Tart

Sweet Libbie's favorite sweet!

CRUST
1 cup flour

¾ cup sliced almonds

¼ cup sugar

¼ teaspoon salt

1 stick unsalted butter, chilled and cut into ½-inch cubes

2 tablespoons heavy cream, chilled

1 egg yolk

CRUMBLE
¾ cup flour

7 ounces almond paste

½ cup light brown sugar

6 tablespoons unsalted butter, chilled and cut into ½-inch cubes

¼ cup sliced almonds

FILLING
12 plums, halved and thinly sliced, or 3 pears, sliced

½ cup sugar

2 tablespoons cornstarch

Blend flour, almonds, sugar and salt in a food processor until almonds are finely ground. Add butter and process until mixture is crumbled. Add cream and egg yolk. Pulse until dough comes together. Press dough over bottom and up the sides of an 11-inch tart pan with a removable bottom. Prick all over with a fork and chill at least 2 hours and up to 1 day.

Preheat oven to 400 degrees.

Bake crust about 25 minutes. If bubbles form while baking, prick with fork periodically. Cool crust on a rack. Reduce oven to 375 degrees

To make crumble, blend flour, almond paste and brown sugar in food processor until almond paste is finely ground. Add butter and blend until coarse crumbs form. Transfer to a bowl and mix in almonds. Sprinkle ¾ cup of crumble over cooled crust.

For filling, combine plums with sugar and cornstarch. Top tart with plums and sprinkle with remaining crumble.

Bake 40 minutes or until filling bubbles thickly and top is golden. Cool on rack.

Port Glazed Walnuts with Stilton

Pears, apples, grapes, crackers, a glass of port, good friends – what better way to end a meal!

2½ cups walnut halves
¾ cup sugar
¾ cup ruby port
½ teaspoon black pepper
1 bay leaf
1 wedge Stilton, Maytag or Roquefort cheese

Preheat oven to 350 degrees.

Toast walnut halves for 10 minutes.

Combine sugar, port, pepper and bay leaf. Cook until slightly thickened.

Add walnuts to port mixture and stir to coat. Drain, reserving ¼ cup liquid.

Spread walnuts on a parchment paper-lined baking sheet. Bake 15 minutes. Cool and separate walnuts, if necessary.

Meanwhile, simmer reserved port liquid over low heat until thick, watching carefully.

Set Stilton on a platter. Drizzle port sauce decoratively over cheese. Surround with fruit and crackers. Serve walnuts in a separate dish.

Pumpkin Flan

SERVES 8-10

Libbie treats us to this delectable flan every Thanksgiving – it is so delicate one can still find room even after the huge main event!

1⅓ cups sugar, divided

¼ cup water

6 eggs

2 cups canned pumpkin

¾ teaspoon salt

½ teaspoon ground ginger

½ teaspoon cinnamon

¼ teaspoon allspice

2 cups heavy cream

Cinnamon-flavored whipped cream

Preheat oven to 350 degrees.

In a small skillet, combine ⅔ cup sugar with ¼ cup water and bring mixture to a boil, stirring and swirling until deep caramel colored. Pour caramel into a 2-quart glass loaf pan, tilting pan to coat bottom evenly. Allow caramel to harden.

In a bowl, beat eggs with remaining ⅔ cup sugar. Add pumpkin, salt, ginger, cinnamon, allspice and cream. Pour mixture into loaf pan and set in a larger pan. Pour boiling water into outer pan to reach halfway up loaf pan.

Bake 2 hours, 15 minutes or until a knife inserted in the center comes out clean. Cool and cover. Chill overnight.

To serve, run a thin knife around sides of pan and invert onto a serving plate. Cut into slices and serve with whipped cream flavored with cinnamon.

Raspberry Chocolate Tarts

SERVES 6

I owe a big thank you to whoever gave me this recipe years ago. Everyone loves it but especially the men!

2 cups walnuts or pecans, toasted

6 tablespoons light brown sugar

¼ teaspoon cinnamon

4 tablespoons butter, melted

¾ cup heavy cream

1 (6-ounce) package chocolate chips

2 baskets raspberries

½ cup seedless raspberry jam, melted

Fresh mint sprigs or chocolate curls for garnish

Preheat oven to 325 degrees.

Combine toasted nuts, brown sugar and cinnamon and grind in a food processor. Add butter and mix well. Press mixture into 6 individual tart pans.

Bake 25 to 30 minutes. Cool on a rack.

Meanwhile, bring cream to a simmer. Remove from heat and stir in chocolate until melted. Cool slightly and pour over baked tart crusts. Chill for several hours.

Arrange raspberries on top of tarts and brush with melted jam.

To serve, remove from pans and decorate with sprigs of fresh mint or chocolate curls.

Rum Cake

Another old classic – this cake gets more delicious if there are any leftovers. Heaven, with a cup of coffee!

BATTER
1 cup chopped walnuts
1 (18-ounce) package yellow cake mix
1 (3-ounce) package instant vanilla pudding mix
4 eggs
½ cup cold water
½ cup canola oil
½ cup dark rum

GLAZE
1 stick butter
¼ cup water
1 cup sugar
½ cup dark rum

Preheat oven to 350 degrees.

Grease and flour a tube or Bundt pan. Sprinkle chopped walnuts over bottom of pan.

Combine cake mix, pudding mix, eggs, cold water, oil and rum in a mixing bowl. Prepare as directed on cake mix package. Pour batter over nuts.

Bake 50 minutes. Cool on a rack. Invert onto a serving plate.

For glaze, melt butter in a saucepan. Stir in water and sugar and boil 5 minutes, stirring constantly. Remove from heat and stir in rum.

Prick top of cake with a wooden skewer. Drizzle and brush glaze evenly over the top and sides of cake.

Tangerine Sherbet

No Chinese feast is complete without a fortune cookie and this grand finale!
This is Amy's specialty!

3 cups tangerine juice
(about 18 tangerines)

Zest from 10 tangerines

¾ cup fresh lemon juice

Zest from 4 lemons

1½ cups Simple Syrup (recipe
below)

¼ cup Mandarin Napoleon or
Grand Marnier liqueur

Mix together all ingredients. Chill for
several hours.

Freeze mixture in an ice cream maker.

SIMPLE SYRUP

2 cups sugar

2 cups water

Combine sugar and water in a saucepan.
Bring to a boil and cook 1 to 2 minutes or
until liquid is clear. Remove and cool.

Triple Lemon Cake

SERVES 12

Calling all lemon lovers! This is it – the perfect cake to serve after a light seafood dinner.

1 package lemon cake mix

FILLING
⅓ cup sugar
1 (8-ounce) package cream cheese, softened
1 egg
2 tablespoons flour
2 tablespoons lemon juice

GLAZE
2 tablespoons lemon juice
1½ cups powdered sugar

Preheat oven to 350 degrees.

Prepare cake batter according to directions on package.

For filling, cream sugar with cream cheese. Beat in egg until fluffy. Add flour and lemon juice.

Pour half of batter into a greased and floured Bundt pan. Cover with cream cheese mixture. Pour remaining batter on top. Gently swirl a knife through batter a few times.

Bake 50 to 60 minutes or until cake pulls away from side of pan. Cool pan in 10 minutes. Invert onto a rack to cool completely.

To make glaze, stir lemon juice into powdered sugar. Drizzle glaze over cooled cake.

A biscotti a day keeps the doctor away! Every Italian knows that.

3¼ cups flour

1 tablespoon baking powder

½ teaspoon salt

1½ cups sugar

1¼ sticks butter, melted

3 eggs

1 teaspoon almond flavoring

1 tablespoon vanilla

2 tablespoons aniseed

1 teaspoon lemon zest

1 cup coarsely chopped blanched almonds, toasted

Preheat oven to 350 degrees.

Combine flour, baking powder and salt in a medium bowl. Combine sugar, melted butter, eggs, almond and vanilla flavorings, aniseed and lemon zest in a large bowl. Add dry ingredients and stir until well combined. Mix in almonds.

Divide dough in half. Using floured hands, shape each half into a long log, 2½ inchs wide. Transfer both logs to a lightly greased baking sheet, spacing logs apart.

Bake logs 30 minutes or until golden brown. Cool logs 10 minutes. Transfer logs to a work surface. Cut logs using a serrated knife (an electric knife works great) on the diagonal into ½-inch thick slices. Arrange slices, cut-side down, on baking sheet.

Bake 12 minutes. Turn biscotti over and bake 8 minutes longer. Transfer to a rack and cool.

Bill's Best Chocolate Chip Cookies

MAKES 16 MEDIUM COOKIES

Bill was in college and he needed cookies so he made them himself! Yum.

2 cups brown sugar
1 stick butter, melted
1 egg
2 cups flour
½ teaspoon salt
½ teaspoon baking soda
½ cup chocolate chips
½ cup butter brickle chips

Add sugar to butter and beat with a fork. Add egg and beat well.

Mix flour, salt and baking soda in a separate bowl. Add dry ingredients to sugar mixture and blend thoroughly. Stir in chocolate and butter brickle chips.

Drop dough by spoonfuls onto an ungreased baking sheet. Bake 10 to 12 minutes.

Breakaway Cookies

A cheese course with fruit and a bit of this cookie is the way to end a meal! So Italian!

½ cup ground almonds
1½ cups flour
½ cup sugar
Pinch of salt
1 tablespoon lemon juice
1½ tablespoons lemon zest
9 tablespoons unsalted butter
1½ tablespoons amaretto liqueur

Preheat oven to 325 degrees.

Combine all ingredients except amaretto. Mix only until crumbly. Sprinkle in the amaretto. Place in an 8-inch cake pan, but do not press down.

Bake 30 to 40 minutes or until lightly golden. Cool on a rack. Cover with foil and let stand one day to mellow.

Guests break apart a piece and pass it along. Hopefully, there is some left by the time it gets to the last person!

Deep Chocolate Cookies

MAKES 3 DOZEN

The song "Deep Purple" has a melody that is haunting and when one hears it you are apt to hum it all the day long. This cookie has the same haunting quality! You will think of it all the day and wish for the time when you will partake of another ecstatic moment!

The deepest chocolate cookie ever!

4 ounces unsweetened chocolate

3 cups semi-sweet chocolate chips, divided

1 stick butter

½ cup flour

½ teaspoon baking powder

½ teaspoon salt

4 eggs

1½ cups sugar

1½ tablespoons instant espresso powder

1 teaspoon vanilla

Melt unsweetened chocolate and 1½ cups chocolate chips in the top of a double boiler. Add butter and stir until smooth. Remove and set aside.

Combine flour, baking powder and salt in a bowl. In another bowl, beat eggs with sugar until thick. Add espresso powder and vanilla.

Fold melted chocolate in egg mixture. Add dry ingredients. Stir in remaining 1½ cups chocolate chips. Refrigerate dough 30 minutes.

Preheat oven to 350 degrees.

Drop by tablespoons onto a parchment-lined baking sheet. Bake 8 to 10 minutes, or until cookies are shiny and cracked on top. Cool on baking sheet and transfer to racks to cool completely.

Empire Biscuits

MAKES 1 DOZEN

This is a long lost recipe of Grandma Reid's which finally surfaced. Libbie and Amy reminisce about these wonderfully delectable, pristine Scottish cookies.

**2 sticks butter, softened
(GR used margarine)**

1 cup sugar

2 egg

3 cups flour

½ teaspoon cream of tartar

½ teaspoon baking powder

Strawberry jam

Powdered sugar

Maraschino cherries

Preheat oven to 350 degrees.

Cream butter with sugar. Add egg and mix well.

Combine flour, cream of tartar and baking powder. Add dry ingredients to creamed mixture.

Roll out dough ¼-inch thick and cut into rounds with a cookie cutter.

Bake 30 minutes, watching that cookies do not become too brown. Cool.

Cover half of the rounds with strawberry jam and top with the remaining rounds.

Mix together powdered sugar with a small amount of hot water to make a thin frosting. Frost the cookies and top each with a maraschino cherry.

The perfect afternoon tea cookie.

Peanut Butter Chocolate Bars

No baking and easier than running to the store for a Reese's candy bar!

- 1 stick butter, melted
- 2 cups graham cracker crumbs
- 2 cups powder sugar
- 1 cup peanut butter
- 1 (12-ounce) package chocolate chips for coating

Blend butter, cracker crumbs, powdered sugar and peanut butter and mix very well. Press into an 11x15-inch pan and chill.

Melt chocolate and spread over surface of bars. Chill again. Cut bars in pan.

Peanut Butter Cookies

For the people who are allergic to flour and for the people who are not allergic to flour!

Quick and easy.

- 1 cup sugar
- 1 egg
- 1 cup chunky peanut butter
- ½ teaspoon vanilla

Preheat oven to 350 degrees.

Mix together all ingredients thoroughly. Drop dough by spoonfuls onto a baking sheet.

Bake 10 minutes, watching carefully. Remove to a rack and cool.

Shortbread

MAKES ABOUT 7-8 DOZEN COOKIES

This is the original family recipe. It is easier now with the food processor. In times past, the dough was kneaded for a long, long time. This method takes 10 minutes to assemble and makes a huge batch!

1 pound butter, softened
1 cup granulated sugar
5½ cups unbleached flour

Preheat oven to 275-300 degrees. (see note below)

Place butter in a food processor and mix until fluffy. Add sugar and process until combined. Add flour, 1 cup at a time, processing after each addition. After about 4 cups of flour are added, turn the dough out onto a board and incorporate the remaining flour with your hands, mixing well.

Place dough in a rimmed baking sheet and press down with a rolling pin until smooth.

Make indentations with the tines of a fork around the edges and prick the dough all over with the fork.

Bake about 1 hour, checking after 50 minutes and baking until the shortbread appears to be very light tan.

Remove from oven. Cut shortbread into even squares and return to the turned off oven. This insures shortbread is cooked all the way through.

None of these instructions are technically explicit – the whole process is accomplished by feel and practice, however, it is not complicated.

It is important to determine how hot your oven bakes. I have used 275 degrees in some ovens, 300 degrees in another.

A 1-inch square is just about right with a wee cup of tea!

Shortbread – Version 2

A great new method of making this favorite cookie. We don't know if our Glasgow Grandmother would approve!

2 sticks butter, melted

1¾ cups flour

½ cup sugar, plus extra for sprinkling on top

¾ cup cornstarch

Preheat oven to 325 degrees.

Mix all ingredients well in a food processor. Press dough into a 9-inch square pan.

Bake 50 minutes. Place pan on a rack and poke shortbread with a fork. Cut into 24 pieces.

Sprinkle with granulated sugar. Remove from pan when cookies are cool.

Oatmeal Cookies Amy

MAKES 3½ DOZEN COOKIES

A collection of our favorites would not be complete without this cookie recipe.

½ cup shortening (makes the cookies crispy)

½ teaspoon salt

2 teaspoons cinnamon

2 teaspoons vanilla

2 tablespoons molasses

1 cup sugar

1 egg

1 cup flour

¾ teaspoon baking soda

1 cup oats

⅓ cup raisins

Preheat oven to 350 degrees.

Combine shortening, salt, cinnamon, vanilla, molasses, sugar and egg in a bowl. Add flour and baking soda and mix well. Add oats and raisins.

Drop dough by level teaspoonfuls onto a greased baking sheet. Bake 15 minutes or until golden brown. Cool on racks.

Swato Cookies

Franni brought these to our annual S.W.A.T.O. meet in Tahoe (Swinging Women's Annual Tennis Outing). Hits the sweet spot every time!

1 (14-ounce) can sweetened
  condensed milk
4 (1-ounce) squares semi-sweet
  chocolate
Pinch of salt
1 teaspoon vanilla
1 cup shredded coconut
¾ cup chopped walnuts

Preheat oven to 350 degrees.

Cook milk and chocolate in the top of a double boiler for 15 minutes, stirring often. Add salt, vanilla, coconut and walnuts.

Place by spoonfuls on a baking sheet. Bake 10 to 12 minutes. Remove from oven and immediately transfer cookies to wax paper.

Cranberry Chutney

Spectacular!

4 cups whole cranberries

2½ cups sugar

1 cup water

6 whole cloves

2 cinnamon sticks

½ teaspoon salt

1 cup golden raisins

2 tart apples, peeled and diced

2 firm pears, peeled and diced

1 small yellow onion, finely chopped

½ cup sliced celery

½ cup chopped walnuts, toasted

1 teaspoon lemon zest

Combine cranberries, sugar, water, cloves, cinnamon sticks and salt in a large saucepan and mix well. Bring to a boil, stirring frequently. Cook 10 minutes or until berries pop.

Add raisins, apple, pear, onion and celery and continue cooking, stirring constantly, for 15 minutes or until thick. Remove from heat and stir in walnuts and zest.

Ladle chutney into jars and refrigerate when cool.

Makes great gifts.

My Marmalade

Toasted English muffins, Irish butter and My Marmalade – Heaven!

2 oranges
1 grapefruit
1 lemon
Sugar

Remove rind from oranges, grapefruit and lemon; setting flesh aside. Remove all white pith from rind. Place rind in a food processor and coarsely chop.

Add flesh from the fruits and pulse until coarsely chopped. This should yield about 2 cups.

Place mixture in a large, wide-mouthed bowl; the wider the bowl, the better. Add an equal amount of sugar to the fruit mixture. Stir until well mixed.

Cook in microwave on high for 15 minutes, stirring occasionally. Marmalade may need to cook an additional 10 minutes – cooking depends on the individual microwave.

Seal in sterilized jars. Cool and refrigerate. Marmalade lasts indefinitely in the refrigerator.

Amy's Red Pepper Jelly

Amy and her pals buy tons of red bell peppers during the season and they all spend the day making this garnet ambrosia! A small amount spread over a block of cream cheese is an instant hors d' oeuvre.

2½ pounds red bell peppers
1 tablespoon salt
1 cup cider vinegar
2 cups sugar

Clean peppers, removing seeds and stem, and coarsely chop in a food processor. Toss with salt and allow to stand 2 hours. Drain well and discard accumulated juice.

Combine bell pepper with vinegar and sugar and bring to a boil. Reduce heat and simmer 1 hour, stirring occasionally. Mixture should be thickened. Cool at room temperature.

Instead of cooking on top of the stove, I have placed all of the ingredients in a wide bowl and microwaved on high for about 15 to 20 minutes or until thickened.

Red Peppers in Oil and Garlic

A colorful addition to any antipasto platter. Can be packed in jars and refrigerated for later use.

Red bell peppers, cut into 3-inch
** wide strips**
Olive oil
Salt to taste
Minced garlic to taste

Place peppers on a large baking sheet. Brush with olive oil and broil until skins blister. Cool and remove peel.

Toss peeled pepper strips with salt and garlic. Serve at room temperature with sliced baguette bread.

Spicy Cranberry Sauce

Goes great with pork, shrimp or chicken.

1 (16-ounce) can jellied cranberry
    sauce
2 tablespoons horseradish
2 tablespoons honey
1 tablespoon lemon juice
2 teaspoons Worcestershire sauce
¼ teaspoon cayenne pepper
1 clove garlic, minced

Combine all ingredients in a saucepan and stir well. Bring to a boil. Reduce heat and cover. Simmer 5 minutes.

Serve warm.

Sweet Mustard

Homemade mustard in minutes.

½ cup dry mustard
½ cup sugar
1 teaspoon salt
2 tablespoons cider vinegar
¼ cup boiling water
¼ cup canola oil
½ cup heavy cream

Combine all ingredients in a blender. Process 1 minute. Scrape down sides and blend 1 minute longer.

Pour mustard into a glass jar and refrigerate at least 24 hours.

Keepers
INDEX

Keepers

CULINARY TREASURES FROM THE HEART

JO DUNBAR SNOW
7458 River Nine Drive
Modesto, CA 95356
209-545-2598

Please send me _____ copies of *Keepers*   @ $22.95 each_____

Postage and handling   @ $ 5.00 each_____

Name _____

Address_____

City _____State _____ Zip _____

Phone Number _____

Make checks payable to: *Jo Dunbar Snow*

- -

Keepers

CULINARY TREASURES FROM THE HEART

JO DUNBAR SNOW
7458 River Nine Drive
Modesto, CA 95356
209-545-2598

Please send me _____ copies of *Keepers*   @ $22.95 each_____

Postage and handling   @ $ 5.00 each_____

Name _____

Address_____

City _____State _____ Zip _____

Phone Number _____

Make checks payable to: *Jo Dunbar Snow*

Keepers

CULINARY TREASURES FROM THE HEART

JO DUNBAR SNOW
7458 River Nine Drive
Modesto, CA 95356
209-545-2598

Please send me _____ copies of *Keepers*   @ $22.95 each _____

Postage and handling   @ $ 5.00 each _____

Name _____

Address_____

City _____ State _____ Zip _____

Phone Number _____

Make checks payable to: *Jo Dunbar Snow*

Keepers

CULINARY TREASURES FROM THE HEART

JO DUNBAR SNOW
7458 River Nine Drive
Modesto, CA 95356
209-545-2598

Please send me _____ copies of *Keepers*   @ $22.95 each _____

Postage and handling   @ $ 5.00 each _____

Name _____

Address_____

City _____ State _____ Zip _____

Phone Number _____

Make checks payable to: *Jo Dunbar Snow*